CZECHOSLOVAKIAN PERFUME BOTTLES

AND
BOUDOIR ACCESSORIES

REVISED EDITION

JACQUELYNE Y. JONES-NORTH

KEN LEACH   RUTH A. FORSYTHE   MADELEINE FRANCE

PHOTOGRAPHY BY DUANE YOUNG, THOMAS NORTH, MORRIS LANE, JAROSLAV KARBULKA, PAT OLSEN, RANDALL MONSEN, AND MADELEINE FRANCE

This book is dedicated to:

Nancy DeRosa
Ruth Forsythe
Madeleine France
Lisa Lippsett
Jill Pence

Description of Back Cover:

A. Opaque green, eight nudes holding a drapery on base, two nudes back to back on stopper, no marks, 7-1/2".

B. Opaque red and black atomizer, six different nude figures dance among glowers, Ingrid design. 7-1/4".

C. Clear and frosted, Young peasant girl in a short dress has her hands on her hips, 7-1/2".

D. Opaque red, all-over poppy design on bottle and stopper, 7-1/4".

E. Blue, nude with flower necklace is standing in a large tulip, 8-1/2".

F. Clear and frosted, flower design/red opaque, Nude touching her hair is sitting on flowers, 6-1/4".

G. Clear and frosted, lady in see-through dress is holding an open fan, 8".

H. Powder box, black opaque, jeweled filigree, pink intaglio handle with an elaborate design of two Egyptian women under a canopy, Hoffman design, 5-3/4".

I. Opaque green, Shy nude in rose stopper, rose filled basket bottle, 6-1/2".

Copyright 1990 by Antique Publications
Revised Edition Copyright 1999 by The Glass Press, Inc.
dba Antique Publications
P.O. Box 553, Marietta, OH 45750-0553

Paperback ISBN# 1-57080-058-8 ◊ Hardback ISBN# 1-57080-059-6

CONTENTS

ACKNOWLEDGEMENTS

To all those who were involved in the making of this book, I owe profound thanks:

Tom Bond, Oklahoma
Nancy and Tom De Rosa, New York
John Dunlap, Ohio
Ruth Forsythe, Ohio
Madeleine and Don France, Florida
Gene Galloway, Texas
Kay Garner, Oklahoma
Debbie Harris, Texas
Linda and Jerry Hemry, Oklahoma
Zita and Charles Hollingsworth, Texas
Justin Jones, Texas
Mary and Roger King, Ohio
Annette Krell, Texas
Janis Knowles, Texas
Ken Leach, New York
Lisa Lippsett, New York
Priscilla McOstrich, New York
Mel Mitchell, Texas
Pauline de Morcia, Texas
Lilly Morgenstern, New York
Jill Pence, Oklahoma
Wayne, Ashley, and Shayne Pence, Oklahoma
Kathy Ratcliffe, Texas
Stephanie Russi, Ohio
Light Tec, Texas
Novatron Lighting, Texas
Jennifer Sgandurra, Ohio
Melvin and Jennifer Traub, Illinois
Margaret and Ken Whitmyer, Ohio
Mary and James Zavada, Texas
Sandy and Bill Holden, Texas

With a special thank you to:

Iris Ascione, Michigan
J. Forester, Texas
Ellen Foster, California
Holly Gilliland, Oklahoma
Janis Helmer, Texas
Linda Neighbors, Oklahoma
Ruth Romberger Johnson, Oklahoma
Donna Sims, Ohio
Jan Smith, Oklahoma
Gloria C. Young, Texas
Wellington Gallery, New York

FOREWORD

The least known or written about glass artisans at the turn of the century and into the '20s and '30s have to be Czechoslovakian mold makers, blowers and polishers. Such names as Hoffmann and Schlevogt are only now being given recognition with such names as Rene Lalique, J. Viard and Lucien Galliard. Nevertheless, the perfume bottles that are known as "Czechs" are among some of the loveliest and most elegant and sensual to be found in eclectic collections of today.

In my years of dealing in these perfume bottles, I have always been amazed at the variety of styles, colors, combinations of stoppers, ormula with semiprecious stones, and glass made to resemble coral, jet, jade, ivory, lapis lazuli and malachite, that are available. I have found them to be enigmatic, original and very difficult to part with. The vibrant colors of the glass bottle matched and perfectly balanced the enormous "figural" stoppers that have not only been exotic but provocatively elegant in the display of the female figure.

As you turn the pages of this book, take a step back in time, and picture the woman who would pick up one of these sensuous bottles filled with her own special essence, carefully chosen to suit her personality, as she dreams about a romantic interlude. The passage of time has allowed these luxurious vessels to survive because they were too beautiful not to keep and display.

In many of the movies done in the "flapper era" and the '30s you will find a "femme fatale" such as Jean Harlow or Carole Lombard using a perfume bottle in her boudoir. DeVilbiss atomizers, Deco Baccarat bottles and Rene Lalique dresser sets are shown sitting on a vanity, but the Czech bottles outshine these not only in their size, but in their sparkling and classical style.

These pages of discovery will bring you into a world that is . . . . for where else is the female form so revered as to be etched in glass or molded for all time . . . . never to be forgotten for its aesthetic beauty.

These Czechoslovakian perfume bottles reflect not only their endurance, but provoke memories of love, charm, and the passion of days gone by, and will remain legendary in their timeless elegance and style.

-- *Madeleine France*
Plantation, Florida

FOREWORD TO THE REVISED EDITION

Written a decade ago, Madeleine France's eloquent words on the preceding page are still true today. While new information on Czech perfume bottles has come to light since 1990, more research is needed. Moreover, what we *have* learned about this subject must be made available to a wider audience.

With this goal in mind, we are pleased to reissue *Czechoslovakian Perfume Bottles and Boudoir Accessories* in a *Revised Edition*. Since going out of print a few years ago, the first edition continues to sell for higher and higher prices at auctions and on the used book market. This ongoing demand tells of the book's worth to dealers and collectors.

Readers will be glad to know that all text and photographs from the original edition have been retained. A 36-page addendum presents three new illustrated articles, as well as an updated price guide.

We are fortunate to have contributions from Ken Leach, Ruth A. Forsythe, and Madeleine France. These individuals are among the most knowledgeable and well-known authorities in the field. They enthusiastically lent their expertise to this project for one main reason: Each felt strongly that Jacquelyne Jones-North's classic book on Czech perfume bottles should be back in print.

In my view, this book should be savored, not scanned. Turn the pages slowly to experience the full mystique and allure of these miniature works of art. You will learn much and enjoy the experience.

--*David E. Richardson*
Publisher

SHORT HISTORY OF CZECHOSLOVAKIA

The history of Czechoslovakia starts with the end of World War I. Czechoslovakia, a country comprising the Czech and Slovak provinces ruled formerly by the Hapsburgs, came into being in 1918 shortly before the capitulation of Austria in World War I. The independence of the new nation was the reward given by the Allied Powers to the Czechs and Slovaks for helping speed the final defeat of the common enemy. The small landlocked nation comprised the ancient kingdoms of Moravia and Bohemia, the Hungarian province of Slovakia, and the Austrian province of Silesia. The country shared common borders with Russia, Poland, Germany, Austria, and Hungary. In 1920, the country adopted a constitution establishing a government modeled on that used in France. Men over 21 and women over 26 had the right to vote. Cultural autonomy and religious equality were guaranteed rights.

The western region of Czechoslovakia, formerly known as Bohemia, had been justly famous for its glass since the 14th century A.D. Bohemian glassmakers, beginning in the early 19th century, produced a flood of products that were exported to other countries including America. When Bohemia became part of Czechoslovakia in 1918 it brought its rich and varied tradition of glass craftsmanship with it. The only thing that really changed were the glass labels which now said "made in Czechoslovakia" instead of "made in Bohemia."

Czechoslovakia, which considered glass-making its national art form, nurtured and encouraged the glass trade. The country funded three schools which taught and improved all aspects of the glass field. For over 20 years fine glass products, including perfume bottles, were manufactured in over 600 glass factories and shipped to countries all over the world. Unfortunately, in 1939, when Hitler and his army invaded Czechoslovakia, the giant glass industry ground to a halt.

BOTTLES

The phenomenal success achieved by the Czechoslovakian crystal perfume bottles in this country between 1928-1939 was richly deserved. The simple to elaborate bottles showed impeccable artistic taste, dazzling beauty, and were of the finest quality, workmanship, and style. The sparkling crystal bottles were hand-cut and polished by skilled artisans who reached for perfection in every small detail. The variety of shapes, colors, and designs produced is overwhelming. The search for bottles to add to a collection could be an enjoyable lifetime pursuit.

The central focal point of many of the bottles was the stopper. Numerous flacons were manufactured with stoppers that were two to three times bottle height to command the attention of the viewer. Some stoppers had designs that matched exactly the designs on the bottles, while others were made that matched only part of the bottle design or did not match at all. The stoppers were individually hand-ground to fit the neck of the bottle. For the stopper to be correct for a bottle, the frosted stopper dowel should fit below the lip of the bottle and be even with the frosted part of the neck.

It became quite clear while viewing advertisements and catalogs of Czechoslovakian bottles that many stoppers were used with more than one style bottle and vice versa. Apparently some companies did not feel that matching a certain style

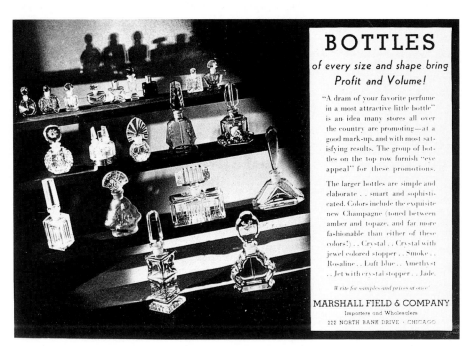

A 1933 Marshall Field & Company advertisement for perfume bottles.

stopper to only one particular bottle was of much importance. This is very noticeable with intaglio and molded figural stoppers. Many of these stoppers never seem to be found very often with the same bottle. This seems to point to the possibility that a few of the importers may have chosen the stopper and bottle combinations that were to be sold as one unit in their separate product lines.

The cut, molded, and intaglio design bottles and stoppers were decorated with an innumerable variety of subjects. A partial list would include geometric designs, scenery, birds, fish, flowers of all types, nudes, children, hunters, cupids, bubble blowers, butterfly women, baskets, 18th-century couples, animals (especially dogs), butterflies, ballerinas, dancers, musicians, and mythological figures. Women in all states of dress and undress were produced, but men, except when part of a couple, were very rarely done. The attractive figural stoppers are normally scarce and usually came in clear and frosted glass. A few of the figural stoppers were tinted to match a bottle color. These stoppers are considered to be hard to find.

The bulk of Czechoslovakian crystal stoppers produced originally came with a dauber, a device for applying the perfume. The devices have also been called drop stoppers, dabbers, and applicators. The dauber is a very narrow glass rod, normally 5/8" to 1-1/4" long, with a pointed, rounded, or ball tip. The dauber was ordinarily a separate piece of glass that was fused to the stopper dowel or tongue. The majority of the daubers were of clear glass, but occasionally some were colored to match the bottle. From time to time a bottle is found with an uncommon extra-long dauber that extends nearly the entire length of the bottle. The two rarest daubers made were a figural and a beaded string. The figural dauber was a three-dimensional nude that could be viewed through the sides of the bottle when the stopper was in place. It has been found in several styles, sizes, and colors. The bead dauber was a string of faceted glass beads attached by the thread to a minuscule glass hoop that was part of the stopper dowel.

The perfume bottles came in a range of sizes to fit the needs and wants of all types of purchasers. The sizes found by collectors can be broken up into four general categories: small (up to 3-1/2"), medium (3-1/2" to 6-1/2"), large (6-1/2" to 8-1/2"), and extra large (8-1/2" and over). The hardest to find size is extra large, and the easiest to find is medium.

Advertisements from the 1930s by various companies offering Czechoslovakian bottles and boudoir accessories often differentiated between regular crystal and lead crystal items. There was a difference, especially in price. A regular crystal perfume bottle might cost a few dollars, while the lead crystal bottle, aimed at the well-to-do, cost substantially more. The rule of thumb during the 1930s for the area of Europe that included Czechoslovakia was that 40% or more lead was used in the lead crystal and 30% less lead was used in the regular crystal. The exact lead content of the crystal would vary from firm to firm. The extra lead in the lead crystal actually added a slight grayish tinge to the clear crystal which many people today find unattractive. If the lead crystal was colored, the tinge is normally unnoticeable.

The low prices charged for the majority of the perfume bottles and boudoir accessories sold in the 1930s should be viewed in the light of the era. The average total family income in the United States in 1939 was $1,231 a year, or $23.67 a week.

Most boudoir items were made to be retailed for no more than a dollar or two. The general population could not have afforded the bottles for themselves or as presents if they had been in a higher price range. One reason for their enormous popularity all through the Depression years was the remarkable high quality and variety offered versus the modest sums charged.

There is an old saying that goes "Imitation is the highest form of flattery." Some of the high-quality Czechoslovakian cut-crystal, relief-molded, and intaglio perfume bottles were imitated by Japanese glassmakers in the 1930s and in the 1940s after World War II. A few of the Japanese flacons are fairly decent copies except for the final finish work done so well by Czechoslovakian craftsmen. The only Japanese bottle I have personally seen with a figural intaglio stopper was such a grotesque duplicate of the original that I laughed until tears came to my eyes. The marked copies are very scarce, so a collector who runs across one should consider adding this unique form of flattery to his or her collection.

See "Japanese Copies," page 82, items 818-820.

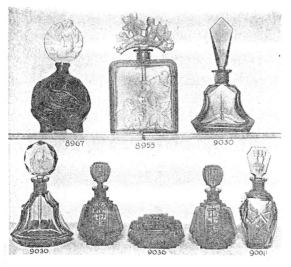

A 1931 advertisement illustrates the large variety of designs available.

8967 8955 9030
9030 9036 9006

SEND FOR OUR NEW CATALOG OF DISTINCTIVE GIFTS FOR MEN AND WOMEN

Imported
PERFUME
BOTTLES

OF hand cut Czecho-Slovakian glass in a large variety of designs and colors. A beautiful new accessory for milady's boudoir.

DISTINCTIVE
SMART
USEFUL

CHARLES L. KING

IMPORTER and MANUFACTURER

260 FIFTH AVENUE   NEW YORK, N. Y.

Established 1920

Just say to advertisers "I saw it in 'The Gift and Art Shop.'"

9

DECORATION

The overwhelming majority of Czechoslovakian crystal bottles and stoppers produced were decorated with hand-cut designs. Simple to very complex geometric patterns were created by combining the three types of cuts that could be made by the skilled laborer—mitre, flat, or hollow cuts. The sparkling designs included an assortment of flutes, fans, stars, diamonds, hexagons, and facet cuts. The cutting was done on a rotating wheel, generally made of iron or steel layered with an abrasive such as damp sand. The final step was to use a felt or wooden polishing wheel to smooth and polish the crystal to a high luster. A type of cutting was also used to shape the crystal blank instead of decorating it. A collector should keep in mind that the more intricate and complex the hand-cut design, the more expensive the bottle or stopper.

Two types of ornamental engraving, wheel-engraving and diamond-point engraving, were occasionally used to decorate the bottles. Wheel-engraving a design on glass involved fine grinding with a small copper wheel turning on a lathe. A pointed hand tool, with a diamond or other hard material at the tip, was used in diamond-point engraving to make light scratches in the surface of the glass. Both techniques were ordinarily used in combination with the cut designs on the bottle.

Czechoslovakian intaglio decoration was a design pressed into glass below the flat surface to leave a reverse relief. !The design was then frequently frosted to better show off the remarkable detail. The edges of the designs were polished by hand as the final step. This process was used mainly for bottle stoppers and other small items. The quite often extra-ordinary designs gave the appearance of expert hand engraving. Some of the stoppers were made with intaglio designs pressed on both sides of the glass. These stoppers are called "double stoppers" by collectors. The glass used for double stoppers was usually twice the thickness of one-sided intaglio stoppers.

Mold-blown bottles and stoppers were made by the relatively simple process of blowing hot glass by hand or machine into a patterned two- or three-part mold that shaped and decorated it in one step. This method allowed the inexpensive production of a large quantity of bottles and other boudoir objects with relief decoration. The careful removal of the cooled glass from the metal forms and the final hand-polishing by

Four types of stoppers compared (l-r): cut crystal, double intaglio, simple intaglio, and molded openwork.

skilled Czechoslovakian craftsmen made these items small masterpieces. The mold-blown flacons can be found in opaque, frosted, and transparent glass. Handsome molded stoppers, many of which were figurals, were often paired with cut-crystal bottle bases. A small number of the molded stoppers were manufactured to show openings through the glass. This type of stopper is called an openworked or pierced stopper.

Jeweled filigree was lace-like ornamental work of delicate or intricate design made of metal set with glass jewels. It was used as a glamorous embellishment on bottles and some other boudoir accessories. Except for purse bottles, less than one bottle in ten can be found sporting this type of decoration. The metal, by and large, came in a gold-tone finish, but once in a while a silver finish is found. The jewels came in a wide range of colors in both transparent and opaque glass. The filigree work on the boudoir flacons was made in both Czechoslovakia and Austria. The Czechoslovakian filigree work was customarily made to fasten around the neck of the bottle by soldering. The filigree made in Austria was normally fashioned so that it could be slipped on and off the base of the bottle fairly easily. "Austria" was usually stamped somewhere on the bottom of the metal piece.

Other decorative techniques used on the bottles were frosting, enameling, and hand painting. A frosted finish was achieved on the outer surface of the glass by exposing it to hydrofluoric acid. Enamel was a substance, colored with pigments derived from metallic oxides, that had a glossy, opaque finish. It was permanently applied by refiring at low temperatures to fuse the enamel with the original surface of the glass piece. Hand painting, also known as cold painting, was the decorative application of lacquer or oil-based colored pigments to the glass without firing. The drawback of this method was that the painted motif could be worn away or easily damaged.

COLOR

All methods of tinting glass throughout history have relied on the skills of the glassmaker and his control over such factors as furnace conditions, the quality of ingredients, and the proportions used. The phenomenal range of colors reached by the very skilled Czechoslovakian glassmakers can be compared to an artist's color wheel. Delicate pastel shades, vivid jewel tones, unusual hues, and opaque colors that rival the richness of semi-precious stones were all produced by these extraordinary craftsmen. There were six basic colors, clear, blue, pink, yellow, green, and purple, manufactured by most of the Czechoslovakian bottle making firms. Each company had its own preferred glass color formulas, so the collector can expect some variations in shade within a basic color group. Also the thinner the glass, the lighter the color will appear to the eye. The rarer colors to be found were the result of careful experimentation combining new materials and proportions by expert artisans.

Each company or importer usually had a fancy trade name for each color of glass it carried which was used in promotions and catalogs. The color yellow for instance was called canary, champagne, or topaz in the advertisements of different companies. Also many collectors have names they prefer to use to describe a glass color. To simplify things in the bottle-grading color chart shown below, I used both the glass color and the alternate trade or collector names for each shade.

The colored bottles that are available to the collector in this country range from the fairly easy to find to the extremely rare. Clear crystal and the other five basic colors are the easiest to collect. The opaque colors are usually the most difficult. Also, there are some transparent or frosted glass colors that were produced that apparently found little favor with the general public at the time and are therefore extremely difficult to locate today. In some cases more bottles were made in a particular color than stoppers and vice versa. An example of this is the glass-color red. It is more difficult to find a red bottle with a clear stopper than a red stopper on a clear bottle. In grading the various glass colors for rarity I took this into consideration and rated the bottles and stoppers separately. In the chart "1" is easiest to find, "2" common, "3" intermediate, "4" scarce, "5" rare, "6" very rare, and "7" hardest to find.

COLOR	BOTTLE	STOPPER	ALTERNATE NAME
Amber	4	4	Gold, Yellowish-Brown
Amberina	7	7	Flame, Red to Yellow
Blue	2	3	Sapphire, Light Blue, Icy Blue, Luft
Blue			
Brown	7	7	Dark Amber
Clear	1	1	Crystal
Cobalt Blue	5	5	Deep Blue
Gray	5	5	Smoke, Charcoal, Transparent Black
Green	2	3	Emerald, Grass Green, Nile Green
Heather	5	5	Pinkish-Purple
Ivory	7	7	White
Opalescent	7	7	Opal
Opaque Black	4	4	Jet, Onyx, Black
Opaque Blue	6	6	Lapis-Lazuli
Opaque Green	5	5	Malachite, Jade
Opaque Orange	7	7	Coral
Opaque Red	6	6	Cinnabar
Opaque Turquoise	7	7	Aqua, Greenish-Blue
Pink	2	3	Rose, Peach, Roseline, Rose Quartz
Purple	3	4	Amethyst, Orchid, Violet, Lavender
Red	5	3	Ruby, Burgundy
Teal	7	7	Blue-Green
Turquoise	7	7	Aqua
Vaseline	5	5	Uranium, Greenish-Yellow
Yellow	3	3	Topaz, Canary, Champagne

COMMERCIAL BOTTLES

Several Czechoslovakian flacons were manufactured to order specifically for commercial use by certain perfume firms. Conde bottled the scent "Dimanche" in a Deco-inspired clear bottle with red painted trim and matching red stopper in the 1930s. Another Deco bottle in lovely peach, cut-glass was used to hold "Forbidden Love" by Le Clairac around 1936. In 1930, Ramses toilet water came in a Czechoslovakian bottle with a very rare nude dauber. The perfume firm Jeurelle used clear cut-crystal flacons for assorted perfumes throughout most of the 1930s. Launched in America in 1934, the French perfume "Triomphe" had a bright red stopper sitting atop a clear, arch-shaped bottle. Dress designer Elsa Schiaparelli and surrealist artist Eleanor Fini collaborated to design the bottle for "Shocking" perfume in 1937. The famous flacons shaped like a dressmaker's dummy were originally made of hand-etched Czechoslovakian crystal. I am positive collectors can find many other commercial bottles made in Czechoslovakia but not mentioned in this book to add to their collections.

See "Commercial Bottles," page 82, items 821-825.

Glass purse bottles covered with elaborate jeweled filigree ornamentation were popular gift items in the 1930s. The screw-on tops, with gold-tone filigree bandings capped with a jewel, came equipped with glass daubers. Many of the filigree patterns were enhanced by touches of delicate enamel work on the metal. Small-scale porcelain or enamel plaques also decorated a few of these ornate containers. The purse bottles range in size from 1-1/2" to 3" and originally retailed for $1.00. Opaque glass purse bottles with molded relief decoration were also marketed in this country. A large number of these molded bottles were manufactured by Ingrid.

In the 1930s women could go to their favorite department store anywhere in America, pick out an attractive little bottle, and have it filled with a dram (one-eighth of an ounce) of a popular or new perfume. To make the expensive imported perfumes affordable for most of their customers, stores would buy the perfume in bulk quantity and salesclerks would dispense it into small bottles made especially for this purpose. The flacons, with screw caps or ground-glass stoppers, usually retailed for 25 cents to 59 cents. Filled with perfume, the total cost was around $1.00 to $1.50. These small bottles were called dram flacons, perfumettes, or miniatures by the importers and wholesalers. Millions of these dram-size bottles sold in this country were made in Czechoslovakia.

Miniatures (minis) were petite cut-crystal dram bottles that were masterful copies of the regular-size boudoir perfume bottles. The only true difference between a small boudoir flacon and a mini is the amount the perfume bottle can hold. Miniatures exhibited all the beautiful details, even ground stoppers with daubers, of the larger bottles. The decoration

A 1932 advertisement.

included frosting, jeweled filigree work, and cut and intaglio designs. The mini bottles came in an array of colors and were 2-1/4" to 4" tall. The bottles were first introduced around 1934 and retailed for 50 cents to 75 cents.

Perfumettes or Lilliputian bottles were dram perfume bottles first introduced to America about 1932. They were made of attractive hand-cut and polished crystal with ground-glass stopper applicators. The perfumettes ranged in size from 2-1/8" to 2-1/2" tall. Irice sold its bottles in individual gift boxes. Many of the dram perfumettes Aristo marketed were close copies of famous commercial perfume bottles of the era, including "Miracle" and "Asphodele" by Lentheric, "Chevalier de la Nuit" and "Surrender" by Ciro, and "Mon Image" by Lucien Lelong. Many of these designs for perfumettes, called Lilliputian bottles by Aristo, were patented by importer Marshall Field & Co. in 1934. The perfumettes normally retailed for 50 cents without perfume.

Crystal dram flacons with screw tops and metal filigree bandings were imported to this country from the mid-1930s. They were promoted in the department stores as the ideal leakproof bottle for the purse.

Most of the dram flacons marketed had tops that were capped with a single glass jewel in assorted colors. Other screw-on-top decorations included seven-pointed jewel stars, marcasite initials on black, multi-color Tyrolean flowers, imitation pearl caps, jewel-studded crowns, and hand-carved roses. The most commonly found flacon is clear and about 2-1/2" tall, but other colors, shapes, and designs were manufactured. A similar screw-top bottle in a half-ounce size was sold as a travelling bottle.

Crystal dram flacons with novel lucky charm tops were sold exclusively by Irice beginning in 1938. They had jewel or filigree screw caps, filigree bandings, elongated glass daubers, 13-millimeter openings, and a single or double charm attached by chains. The cute charms included miniature boys and girls, fruit, elephants, shoes, hearts, single beads, four-bead dangles, cones, and dice. An initial charm, a metal letter set with stones, also was sold. The charms were made in clear, blue, green, purple, red, yellow, and gay multi-color glass. The charm bottles were wholesaled for $21.60 a gross or 15 cents apiece.

See "Purse, Dram, and Mini Bottles," pages 67-70, items 597-698.

TWIN SETS

As part of her personal signature, the average woman of today has a single brand of perfume she prefers to wear most of the time. The fashionable woman of the 1920s and 1930s, however, was urged by the style setters of the era to use a different perfume for each mood, occasion, costume, and the time of day. To cash in on this fad, twin sets and clusters were marketed by such companies as Irice, Premiere, and Aristo. The sets came complete with two to four bottles and a tray holder. Usually the stoppers and

trays were matching colored cut crystal, while the bottles were clear crystal. Some of the three-bottle clusters Aristo produced came in three different sizes. Irice also marketed inexpensive four-bottle sets, with screw tops in metal filigree holders. The two- to four-bottle sets retailed for $1.00 to $1.95. The easiest ones to locate are the twin sets with two bottles. The three- and four-bottle clusters are very difficult to find complete with all the matching pieces.

See "Twin Sets," page 71, items 699-704.

ATOMIZERS

An atomizer works by reducing the perfume to a fine spray by mechanical means using air. The atomizer transforms a single small drop of perfume into hundreds of tiny scented droplets. The heyday of the atomizer was the 1920s, and millions of them were sold in this country alone. Numerous mold-blown atomizer bottles in an immense assortment of styles made in Czechoslovakia were marketed in this country. Many importers and atomizer companies, such as George E. Migon Inc., Maurice Levy, Debans Importing Corp., DeVilbiss, and Marcel Franck, included Czechoslovakian-made atomizer bottles in their product line along with bottles made elsewhere in Europe and the United States.

In 1936, DeVilbiss patented and marketed a line of cut-crystal atomizers that were designed by Frederic A. Vuillemenot and manufactured in Czechoslovakia. This line of atomizers blended beautifully with the crystal boudoir items sold by other companies. The bottles came in crystal, blue, pink, green, yellow, and topaz glass. The popular line was imported by DeVilbiss until 1939. By and large, these atomizers were acid-marked and carried a paper DeVilbiss label.

See "Atomizers," pages 71-72, items 705-727.

BOUDOIR ACCESSORIES

The immense success of the Czechoslovakian cut-glass perfume bottles in the American marketplace had the importers and manufacturers scrambling to discover other boudoir items to tempt the consumer's pocketbook. Catalogs, magazines, and whole-sale and retail advertisements revealed a surprisingly long list of boudoir accessories that were definitely sold in this country. The list includes:

Perfume bottles
Cologne bottles
Atomizers
Powder boxes
Dresser trays
Perfume lamps
Cotton dispensers
Tissue boxes
Puff-patters
Water goblets
Solid perfume containers
Toilet or bathroom bottles
Talcum shakers
Hand mirrors
Magnifying mirrors
Rouge containers
Pin trays
Clocks
Lighters
Cream jars
Trinket boxes
Ashtrays
Dresser sets
Vanity sets

In 1932, Irice started a new trend by marketing in this country magnifying mirrors that had Czechoslovakian crystal handles with cut or intaglio designs. The patterns on the handles duplicated the colors and designs of many of Irice's perfume bottles and powder boxes. The crystal handle was attached to the mirror back with a metal swivel attachment. The inserts on the back of the mirrors included flower or Watteau prints and cloisonne in a full range of pastel colors. Some of the mirrors sold had mirrors on both sides instead of an insert. A few were made with a glass medallion attached to the back that matched the handle. The enormous success that Irice had with the mirrors spurred other companies to include them in their product lines.

Perfume lamps were small lamps, usually under six inches tall, made with a shallow indentation in the top of the glass shade. The user poured a small amount of perfume or cologne into the indentation and the heat from the lighted bulb would slowly evaporate the contents, scenting the room. The dainty lamps, which came complete with bulb, socket, plug, and six feet of wire, were also advertised for use as night lights. The lamps were made of cut crystal, polished glass, or of frosted glass with hand-painted decorations. The popular lamps were marketed throughout most of the 1930s in this country. The polished glass and frosted glass lamps usually cost around $1.00. The heavily cut crystal lamps and those with hanging crystal pendant decorations ranged in cost from $2.00 to $6.50.

A charming item sold in the late 1930s in America was the puff-patter. A fine-quality French swansdown powder puff was attached to a Czechoslovakian cut-crystal handle. The handles came in clear crystal and other assorted pastel colors. The puff-patters were designed to match perfume bottles and magnifying mirrors sold by the same company. Regretfully, I have only seen examples of the puff-patters shown in advertisements. The collector who finds one will have a truly unique addition to his or her collection.

Cotton dispensers, also called cotton pickers, have often in the past been mistaken by both collectors and dealers for broken bottles. The dispensers came in several shapes but always had a circular opening at the side or top. They were available in cut-crystal and satin glass in an assortment of colors. The dispensers, priced to retail for $1.00 or less, originally came packed with cotton. Marketed by several firms, the cotton dispensers first appeared in the United States in the mid-1930s.

Coordinated toilet or bathroom sets in cut-crystal and pressed glass were distributed by several companies. The various sets marketed came with three or more matched pieces. A set could include such items as a cotton dispenser, water goblet, powder box, cream jar, and bottles to hold cologne, mouthwash, lotion, peroxide, or boric acid. The bottles usually had wider necks than perfume bottles and the stoppers were flat bottomed, without daubers. An unusual four-piece, cut-crystal bathroom set sold by De Boer and Livingston in 1937 boasted cut and polished name plates designating the contents suspended from the necks of the bottles by fine linked chain. The most expensive set I have seen pictured was a 1936 Irice import of heavily cut lead crystal with three bottles of graduated sizes, a powder box, and a box to hold cream. The set retailed for $35.00.

In 1936, three-piece dresser sets consisting of a brush, a hand mirror, and a comb were marketed by Irice and Premier. The backs of the brush and mirror were ornamented with artistic cut or intaglio glass inserts. The baroque metal handles were usually gold-plated. The sets were very costly and retailed for $20 to $25. In 1937, Morlee introduced dresser sets with matching handles made of beautiful hand-cut Czechoslovakian crystal in many different designs. The cloisonne backs came in ivory, blue, green, peach, or black framed by engine-turned metal with a silver or gold finish. The average price for a set was $5.95. Irice and Premier also sold these lower-priced sets beginning in 1938. Many companies sold the dresser mirrors with cut or intaglio handles as individual items. In 1938, Irice marketed a dresser mirror with crystal handle that retailed for $1.00. It had a delicate chased-bronze frame ornamented with enameled and jeweled filigree designs.

The Czechoslovakian cut-crystal powder boxes and dresser trays came in a rainbow of colors like the perfume bottles. While the perfume bottles came in hundreds of patterns, the powder boxes and trays have been found in only a few dozen designs. The boxes, bottles, and trays were ordinarily sold as separate pieces, not as sets. The customer or store owner would usually pick out individual pieces in matching colors to make up a coordinated ensemble. The crystal boxes ranged in price from $1.00 to $7.00 and the dresser trays from $6.00 to $25.00.

Three-piece Czechoslovakian vanity sets, which included two bottles and a powder box in the same pattern, were offered here by several companies in the mid-to-late 1930s. The majority of the sets manufactured were aimed at the multitude of price conscious consumers with modest means. These sets, made of pressed glass with a polished or satin finish, retailed for $1.00 to compete with the inexpensive depression-glass sets made by glass firms in the United States. A few of the sets originally came with a simple mirror plateau. The dollar vanities can be found in several colors, including clear, pink, blue, green, and amber. In 1938 Irice promoted a $1.00 vanity set, with vase-and-flower-design intaglio stoppers, which the advertisement claimed was half-solid crystal. After reading over the ad carefully, I came to the conclusion that only the stoppers were crystal, that the box and the bottles were actually pressed glass. On the other end of the scale, the top of the line cut or engraved sets were very expensive for the time period. The suggested retail price of a luxurious matched lead-crystal set was between $25.00 and $35.00.

Talcum shakers were introduced by Irice and other companies in about 1936. They looked like extra-large salt shakers and came in assorted colors of cut crystal. Also introduced by Irice in 1936 were jeweled, cut-glass rouge pots which were made in several shades. The small, square rouge containers are similar in size and shape to the solid perfume holders. The rouge pots were also marketed in a small circular shape. A 1937 advertisement featured an elaborate tissue box marketed by De Boer and Livingston. It was trimmed with mirror plate and had cut and polished crystal squares inserted in the top of the box. I am sure other Czechoslovakian tissue boxes were sold in this country. A sparkling, cut-crystal cigarette lighter was offered by Morlee in 1938 as an unusually attractive table or boudoir accessory. That firm's collection of lighters harmonized with its crystal toiletries ware. Pretty cut-crystal clocks started showing up in the wholesale ads of several companies in 1936. The retail prices for the clocks were between $5.00 and $7.50. Boudoir clocks with intaglio decoration were also manufactured. Sometimes only the crystal cases were made in Czechoslovakia, while the clockworks were produced in another European country or the United States.

See "Boudoir Accessories," pages 73-79, items 728-802.

IMPORTERS, MANUFACTURERS, AND TRADE NAMES

Czechoslovakian glass of all types flowed into this country soon after the end of World War I. It was not until 1928, though, that the beautiful cut-crystal bottles began to appear in gift shops and department stores. Two firms, Koscherak Bros. Inc. and Morlee, were among the first companies to attempt to mass market the bottles to the American public. Koscherak Bros., started in 1887, were importers of European products, especially Bohemian glass—including that produced by Egermann. Other companies soon began to import the attractive bottles to satisfy the enormous demand for them by the public. Irice, the Irving W. Rice Co. of New York, started selling the cut-crystal bottles and dresser accessories in 1931. In 1934 the A.J. Linke

Co. of New York became the factory representative in the United States for Meyer's Nephew, Ltd. of Adolf, Czechoslovakia, which manufactured toilet sets and other glassware. The A.J. Linke Co. also represented Associated Glass Furnace, Ltd. of Kasten, Czechoslovakia, which also manufactured glassware. In 1931, an advertisement for the importer Charles L. King showed that his firm imported and wholesaled in America the fine perfume bottles made by the Hoffman company in Gablonz, Bohemia. The Simfred Co. of New York pictured in a 1933 wholesale ad the Beckhard line of frosted glassware called "Lareine." The line included a relief-molded, black or white glass perfume bottle made in Czechoslovakia.

It is a sad fact that little or no information is currently available about the many companies that imported or manufactured the cut-crystal bottles and accessories between 1928-1938. After much research I have attempted to compile a list of as many of the makers, importers, and trade names as possible.

The list includes the following:

A.J. Linke, N.Y.
Aristo
Charles L. King, N.Y.
Czecho-Slovak Glass Prod. Co., N.Y.
De Vilbiss
E & J P
E & T B
Edward G. Westlake, Chicago
Edward P. Paul, N.Y.
Friedlaender & Co., L.A., N.Y., Chicago
Heinrich Hoffman
Importer's Guild, Inc., N.Y.
Ingrid
Irice-Irving W. Rice, N.Y.
Jones Co., Chicago
Josef Inwald A.G.
Koscherak Bros. Inc., N.Y.
McCoy, Jones & Co., Chicago
McCoy, Jones & Westlake, Chicago
Marshall Field & Co., Chicago
Meyer's Nephew, Ltd.
Morlee
Nasco
Paris Decorators
Paul A. Straub & Co., N.Y.
Premier Co., N.Y.
Simfred Co., N.Y.

THE BUTTERFLY MARK AND THE INGRID LABEL

Heinrich Hoffman was one of the foremost designers of Czechoslovakian perfume bottles and other glass in the 20th century. Hoffman, and later his son-in-law, Henry Schlevogt, greatly influenced the Bohemian glass industry with their new ideas, designs, and methods. Heinrich was the son of Franz Hoffman who owned a company in Marschowitz, Bohemia, that made glass jewelry. Having learned much about the glass trade from his father, Heinrich Hoffman opened a glass firm in Paris on the Rue de Bretagne before 1900. Around 1900, Hoffman also founded a glass firm in Gablonz, Bohemia, not far from Marschowitz. The sister companies had only one aim, to produce artistic, well-designed, and executed pressed glass products for the

market place. The signature used by Hoffman on his marked glass pieces was a small open-winged butterfly molded into the glass. Often in the past this signature has been mistaken for a similar mark used by the famous glass firm of Thomas Webb & Sons of Stourbridge, England. *See "Hoffman Glass," pages 80-81, items 803-813.*

The town of Gablonz, in Northern Bohemia near the present-day town of Ceska Lipa, was an excellent choice by Hoffman for a glass firm. It was a major center for the glass industry in Bohemia before World War II and was famous for its beautifully crafted products, including beads, buttons, and fake gems. A large pool of skilled employees was available there for the company. The recorded population in

1910 for Gablonz was 29,605, out of which over 12,000 were workers in the glass trade.

Hoffman resided and designed his glass in Paris, at that time the art capital of the world. His designs were deeply inspired by art nouveau, art deco, Greek and Roman mythology, and, later, the work of the famous designer Rene Lalique. The glass molds used to make his imaginative designs a reality were fashioned in Gablonz. While Hoffman lived and designed for his firm in Paris, his intelligent, energetic wife, Josephine, managed the business side of the firm in Gablonz. It was a great blow to Hoffman and the company when Josephine died in the 1920s.

An interesting sideline of the Hoffman factory was the manufacture of artificial human eyes used to replace ones lost by war, disease or accident. The glass eyes were considered to be of a very high standard for that era. Austrian Emperor Franz Joseph II acknowledged this accomplishment by awarding Heinrich Hoffman a high title.

During the mid-1920s, Heinrich Hoffman pioneered a new method of pressing glass. The design was pressed as a negative from the reverse side into the glass, then frosted. This made the finished piece look like really fine cut glass. Collectors of Czechoslovakian glass today call this form of decoration "intaglio cutting." With this new process the company produced perfume bottle stoppers, ashtrays, pin trays, clock cases, box lids, handles for mirrors and powder puffs, etc. The expert craftsmanship of the molds, skillful removal of the glass forms, and the final meticulous hand-polishing of the edges made these tasteful, elegant objects a work of art.

Most of the pressed pieces were really manufactured by the glass firm of Walter Riedel in Polnan, Czechoslovakia. Vases with figures in relief and small sculptures of glass were also made in Polnan. Very gifted artists of the time designed for the farsighted Heinrich Hoffman. They included Adolf Becker (director of a special glass school), Alexander Pfohl (Professor at the Work School of Haida), Professor Zdenek Juna, and Professor Joseph Drahonovsky and his pupil Frantisek. Frantisek later worked for the Hoffman firm as one of its leading designers.

In the late 1920s, Hoffman's daughter, Charlotte, married Henry G. Schlevogt. He was the son of Curt Schlevogt of Gablonz who owned a factory that produced buttons and Venetian-type glass jewelry. Henry Schlevogt worked for several years for the Hoffman firm developing his natural talent for glass design and formulation. While working for the company, Henry created new molds and originated certain rich stone-like pressed glasses which resembled lapis lazuli and jade. Schlevogt went back to his own firm in 1930 after the sad and unexpected death of his young wife following the birth of their only child, Ingrid Charlotte. Heinrich Hoffman bestowed on Henry when he left the company several important molds and the whole production of the lapis and jade glass, which was still being developed. Some of the Hoffman firm's mold makers and glass artists followed Henry to his company. The gift of several molds designed by Hoffman explains the appearance of occasional butterfly marks in the glass produced by Schlevogt.

Henry Schlevogt worked for many years to develop glasses that had all the depth and richness of semi-precious stone. The process was finally perfected to his satisfaction in 1934. Henry unveiled his new collection of lapis and jade glass along with his regular glass line at a famous trade fair in Leipzig, Germany. To bring the entire collection luck, Schlevogt used the trade name and mark "Ingrid," after his small daughter of that name. At the age of only 30, Schlevogt achieved great success with his remarkable Ingrid glass line that was marketed internationally. Today many of the most beautifully crafted Czechoslovakian perfume bottles and accessories found by collectors have the Ingrid paper label or acid mark. *See "Ingrid Glass," page 81, items 814-817.*

The glass that Schlevogt's firm produced far exceeded the glass made by his father-in-law, Heinrich Hoffman. Some of

Schlevogt's glass designs reflected the art noveau tradition, others the newer art deco style, and still other the austere Bauhaus fashion. For the next five years Schlevogt commissioned well-known artists and craftsmen to design for Ingrid in order to keep the quality of the glass on the highest possible level. They included Eleon von Rommel from Berlin, Professor Zdenek Juna from Eisenbrod, Valley Wieselthier from New York, Professor Arthur Plewa from Gablonz, Professor Bruno Mauder in Zwiesel, Mario Petrucci, Ena Rottenberg, Hagenaur and Ida Schetz-Lehmann from Vienna. Schlevogt's second wife, Margaret Scheibler, also contributed to the company by using her discriminating eye to judge what final designs should be produced for the collection.

The beginning of World War II in Europe in 1939 tragically brought to a close the Hoffman and Schlevogt era in glass. Heinrich Hoffman, by then an old man, died in Paris. Schlevogt fled to Czechoslovakia, leaving behind his life's work, including his glass molds. In 1950, Henry Schlevogt finally settled in Paris and started the Cristallerie du Val d'Andelle in the Rue de Paradise. In Czechoslovakia Schlevogt's firm, ideas, and glass molds were practically stolen from him.

After the end of World War II many of the molds designed or commissioned by Schlevogt were again put to use by glass firms controlled by the Communist government. The beauty, the precise quality of the molding, and the meticulous hand-polishing demanded by Schlevogt are largely absent from the products made after the war. Until recently, the new regime made jade glass, but the beautiful lapis glass was never again attempted. At this time only clear and frosted glass versions of some of Schlevogt's molds are being produced in small quantities in Czechoslovakia. Thus, the older pieces will always be eagerly sought by the knowledgeable collector.

MARKS

As a rule most Czechoslovakian crystal or mold-blown perfume bottles, clocks, atomizers, and powder boxes, etc. made between 1918 and World War II were signed with an acid-etched mark. The acid stamp can be found in a variety of shapes, sizes, and spellings that basically say "made in Czechoslovakia" or just "Czechoslovakia." The Hoffman glass company marked many of its pieces with a small open-winged butterfly, sometimes hidden in the bottle design pattern, on the stopper dowel, or near intaglio decoration. Some crystal items also had the name of the maker or importer—for example, Paris Decorator, Ingrid, or Irice—acid-etched on the glass. The mark on a perfume bottle is most commonly found on the bottom, but on occasion one can be seen marked on one of the bottle's sides. Acid marks on powder boxes can be located on the bottom and inside the box base. At times, only part of an acid mark is discovered on crystal powder boxes, bottles with cut bottoms, and bottles with feet.

Every so often, a bottle or other boudoir item has an acid mark so faded, worn, or faint that it is difficult to find. To find it, first try holding the bottom at different angles to your eye under a very strong light. If that fails, try bringing the acid back to the surface by rubbing the bottom of the piece briskly on a piece of denim or a bath towel until warm to the touch. This will sometimes bring the acid to the glass surface for a few short moments. Frost the mark by breathing immediately on the surface.

The cologne bottles and pressed-glass

boudoir items were routinely signed with an embossed or molded mark on the bottom. These marks will project slightly from the surface of a piece. At times, these items have been seen marked with a painted, ink, or acid stamp. Purse bottles customarily carried a small metal plate stamped "Czechoslovakia" fixed on the screw tops or attached to the filigree work. Many atomizers were signed with an engraved mark on the metal fittings or a normal mark on the bottom of the glass.

It is truly amazing to me that so many Czechoslovakian boudoir accessories still have the original trademark or importers' labels affixed to them. These paper labels, usually gold or silver, can be a valuable clue to the origin of a piece when the normal mark is difficult to find. When a collector finds an item with a paper label, it should be left intact.

WORLD WAR II - 1980s

When Czechoslovakia was invaded by Nazi Germany in 1939, it became subject to the ruthless exploitation of its resources and industries, and the brutal oppression of its people. Supplies of glassware, including perfume bottles, were no longer available to the United States. Some farsighted importers, such as the Koscherak Bros. Inc. and Paul A. Straub and Co., had seemingly anticipated the coming shortage and prudently stockpiled a supply of Czechoslovakian glassware in American warehouses. Advertisements for Czechoslovakian-made glassware placed by Paul A. Straub and Co. appeared as late as 1942.

In most cases the many importers of Czechoslovakian glass were caught short by the war and had to turn to other sources for products to sell. Irice and Morlee turned to American glass factories to produce hand-cut and polished crystal perfume bottles, trays, magnifying mirrors, clocks, and powder boxes in the Czechoslovakian style. The imitations made and sold in the United States during the war years came in a very limited range of colors: clear, pink, blue, and, sometimes, amber. Two of the firms that supplied Irice with bottles were the Imperial Art Glass Co. of Bellaire, Ohio, and Gundersen-Pairpoint Glass of New Bedford, Mass.

It is interesting to note that several American glass companies during the early 1940s advertised products made by transplanted Czechoslovakian craftsmen, including the Silverbrook Art Glass Co. of Riverhead, N.Y., and the Cavalier Glass Co. of Long Island City, N.Y. Apparently, many Czechoslovakians trained in the glass trade fled their country during this difficult period in its history and resettled in the United States. A 1940 Irice advertisement picturing two beautiful bottles, a powder box, and a tray stated that they were "made in an American Factory by artisans who for years operated the largest perfume bottle manufactory in Czecho-Slovakia." Unfortunately, neither the names of the artisans or the factories were mentioned in the ad copy.

Several other companies sold boudoir accessories patterned after Czechoslovakian items during World War II. The list includes Art Glow Creations, Block Mfg. Co., American Cut Crystal Corporation, M.B. Daniels and Co., Edward P. Paul and Co., and L. Luria and Son. In 1940 the "Paulus" line of perfume bottles was sold by Edward P. Paul and Co. of New York. The line included American-made reproductions of Czechoslovakian and Swedish perfume bottles, trays, and powder boxes of heavy polished crystal. The Block Mfg. Co. of Chicago also manufactured crystal perfume bottles and boxes beginning in 1940. Starting around 1941, the American Cut

Crystal Corporation made hand-cut and polished crystal ware, including perfume bottles, lighters, ashtrays, and powder and cigarette boxes. L. Luria and Son of New York marketed a line of boudoir items in both pressed and mold-blown glass under the trade name "Luraline" beginning around 1944. The only colors mentioned in their ads were clear and ruby glass. Art Glow Creations of New York sold American hand-cut and hand-decorated bottles and powder boxes under the "Wondercraft Glassware" trademark in the mid-1940s. The bottles came in peach, green, and frosted glass.

By 1943, the most pressing problem in the entire American glass industry was the steady loss of both skilled and unskilled labor. Complicated cut and etched patterns were withdrawn by most manufacturers to meet the many limitations caused by the war in both production and distribution. The complex Czechoslovakian-type imitations slowly disappeared from the marketplace to be replaced with simpler boudoir items in a limited selection.

With the end of World War II in 1945 four things hampered the resurgence of the Czechoslovakian glass industry as a world leader: the steady loss of skilled workers, the destruction of many glass factories during the War, the Communist control of the industry, and the changing tastes of the buying public.

Between the late 1930s and 1946 the large pool of skilled glassworkers in Czechoslovakia was slowly evaporating due to death and emigration to other countries to escape the horrors of war. Many artisans of German descent living in Czechoslovakia were relocated to Germany right after the war under the Marshall plan. They took their vast experience in the glass trade with them. Many crystal bottles found today marked "made in Germany" were actually made after the war by resettled Czechoslovakian-trained glassworkers. The DeVilbiss company was a large buyer of the bottles these craftsmen produced.

In 1946, the new Communist regime in Czechoslovakia consolidated the 58 glass factories that survived the war into only 15

companies. The glassware manufactured by these firms was marketed by a government agency called GLASSEXPORT, a shortened version of Czechoslovak Glass Export Company, Ltd. The agency must have stifled or discouraged innovation and originality. The crystal bottles made in Czechoslovakia

IMPORTED
*Sparkling Crystal,
Hand Cut*

PERFUME BOTTLES

from Czechoslovakia

One of many new items in our recent shipment. See our complete line at the Chicago Gift Show, Aug. 4th to 16th, at the Palmer House.

IMPORT
Products Company
841 W. CERMAK RD.
CHICAGO 8, ILL.

An advertisement in Crockery and Glass Journal *for July 1947.*

since the war are frequently inferior copies of the 1930s bottles; the quality of the glass is lower, there is more pressed than cut decoration, and hand-finishing is virtually nonexistent. The molded bottles with relief decoration manufactured after the war were by and large produced from molds originally made in the 1920s and 1930s. Only two colors of molded bottles are known to have been made since the war, opaque green and frosted glass. All the newer bottles were not acid-marked. They normally only have a paper label with "GLASSEXPORT" or "Bohemian glass made in Czechoslovakia" printed on them.

In America in 1946 and 1947, Irice, Importers Guild of New York, and Import Products Company of Chicago seemingly imported bottles from Czechoslovakia made prior to World War II. The cut-crystal bottles shown in the ads look to be the older 1930s type, instead of the simplified versions that were customarily made after the war. The three importers probably found a supply of boudoir items that had been in storage in Czechoslovakia all through the conflict.

Even though several companies tried to reintroduce Czechoslovakian bottles to the American public in the mid-to-late 1940s, they were not successful. The taste of the average consumer had changed. Early American and Danish modern styles became the fashion of that era. The typical retailer could sell plenty of milkglass, hobnail, and simple, modernistic-style bottles, but the pretty, highly cut, colored crystal bottles were considered old-fashioned and no longer in demand.

In 1949, GLASSEXPORT took out one advertisement in an American trade journal that pictured four pieces of opaque green glassware, including an atomizer and perfume bottle, that displayed paper "Ingrid" labels on them. The advertisement stated that they were made by the JABLONEC CRYSTALLERY in Czechoslovakia. The molds used were made prior to World War II.

In the later 1950s, GLASSEXPORT again made the hand-finished, opaque green, molded-relief glassware available to the American market. The extensive collection of opaque green glass made from 1930s molds was called "Jade" glass by the agency in advertisements and catalogs. Twenty-two different vanity sets, commonly consisting of a perfume bottle, atomizer, powder box, and pin tray, were offered for sale. Some sets were alike except for the bottle stoppers used. Nine assorted purse bottles and other individual boudoir pieces were also produced. These items were not acid marked and only carried a paper label. Today this glassware made in the 1950s is sought after.

In the early 1970s (until 1977), Weil Ceramics and Glass Inc. of New York imported a line of clear and frosted glass from Czechoslovakia under the name "BAROLAR SCULPTURE GLASS." The line included four vanity sets and two single bottles. Once more, many of the older molds were used. The frosting on this glass is not of the high standard of the older glass. The line did exceptionally well in this country and for unknown reasons was discontinued for export by the Czechoslovakian glass agency in 1977.

In the mid-1980s, a small run of opaque green glass was made available in the United States by GLASSEXPORT. Only a small number of items were available compared to the extensive offering in the late 1950s. GLASSEXPORT now exports to this country only clear and frosted glassware made from the older molds.

See "Contemporary Bottles," page 82, items 826-829.

COLOR ILLUSTRATIONS

*(Multiple items in the photographs
that follow are always identified left
to right.)*

1. Clear and frosted/frosted opaque black, molded rose design, 4-1/8".

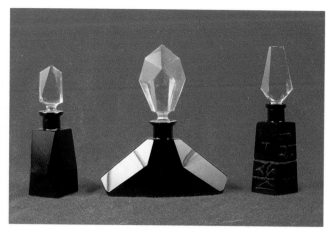

2. Clear/opaque black, 4-3/4".
3. Clear/opaque black, 5-1/2".
4. Clear/opaque black, 5-1/2".

5. Clear/opaque black, 3-5/8".
6. Clear/opaque black, 4-1/2".
7. Clear/opaque black, 3-3/4".

8. Clear/opaque black, 4-1/4".
9. Clear/opaque black, 5-1/2".
10. Clear/opaque black, 4".

11. Clear and frosted/opaque black, 5".
12. Clear/opaque black, 4-1/2".
13. Clear/opaque black, 5-1/4".

14. Opaque black and frosted/clear and frosted, 3-5/8.
15. Opaque black/clear and frosted, 5".
16. Opaque black/clear and frosted, 5-3/4".
17. Opaque black/clear, 3-3/4".

18. Clear/opaque black, 4".
19. Clear/opaque black, jeweled filigree, 4-1/4".
20. Clear/opaque black, 4-1/8".

21. Clear/opaque black, 5".
22. Clear/opaque black, 6-1/2".
23. Clear/opaque black, 5-1/2".

24. Clear/opaque black, 5-3/4".
25. Clear and frosted/opaque black, jeweled filigree, 8-1/8".
26. Clear/opaque black, 5-5/8".

27. Clear and frosted, prancing nude with drapery is playing a flute, 5-1/2".

28. Clear and frosted, portrait of a woman/pink, 5-5/8".

29. Frosted, gray staining/opaque red, gray staining, molded sunflower design, 6".

30. Blue, 4-1/2".
31. Clear and frosted/blue, 6-1/4".
32. Blue, 4-1/2".

33. Pink, 5-1/8".
34. Pink, 4-3/8".
35. Pink, 4-5/8".

36. Blue, 5".
37. Blue, 6".
38. Blue, 5-1/8".

39. Clear/blue, 3-1/4".
40. Clear/blue, 5-3/8".
41. Clear, 2-1/2".

42. Blue/clear, 4".
43. Blue/clear, 6-1/2".
44. Blue/clear, 3-7/8".

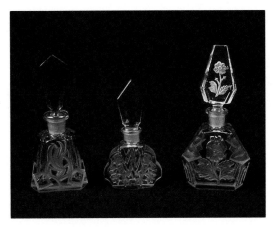

45. Blue, 5".
46. Blue, 4".
47. Clear and frosted/blue, 5-1/4".

48 (Right). Clear and frosted, Grecian woman holding a baton over head/yellow, 5-1/2".

49 (Far right). Clear and frosted, pink staining, two flamingos under palm tree with fish in water/green, mismatched bottle and stopper, 7-7/8".

50. Yellow, 3-3/4".
51. Clear and frosted/yellow, 4".
52. Yellow/clear, 3-1/2".

53. Yellow, 4-1/2".
54. Clear/clear and frosted, jeweled filigree, 4-1/8".
55. Yellow, 4-1/8".

56. Clear/yellow, 6".
57. Yellow, jeweled filigree, 6-1/2".
58. Clear and frosted/yellow, 5-3/4".

59. Amber, 3-3/4".
60. Amber, 3-3/4".
61. Amber, 3".

62. Amber, 4-3/4".
63. Amber, 4-1/2".
64. Frosted/amber, 5".

65. Green/clear, 7-1/8".
66. Green/clear, 5-1/4".
67. Green/clear, 6".

68. Green, 5".
69. Green, 5".
70. Green, 5-1/8".

71. Green, 4".
72. Green, 5-1/4".
73. Green, 4-1/2".

74. Green, 4-1/4".
75. Green, 3-3/4".
76. Green, 4-1/4".

77. Green, 4-1/2".
78. Green, 4-3/4".
79. Green, 4-7/8".

80. Green, 5-1/8".
81. Yellow, 5".
82. Green, 5".

83 (Right). Red opaque/black opaque, parrot perched on branch, 5-5/8".

84 (Far right). Red opaque, tiara stopper/ black opaque, 5-5/8".

85. Gray, 4-1/2".
86. Clear/gray, 3-1/2".
87. Gray, 4".

88. Pink, 5-1/2".
89. Clear and frosted/pink, 7-3/4".
90. Pink, 4-3/4".

91. Red/clear, 5-1/4".
92. Red/clear, 6-1/2".
93. Red/clear, 5-5/8".

94. Red/clear and frosted, 4-3/4".
95. Red/clear and frosted, 5".
96. Red/clear, 4-3/4".

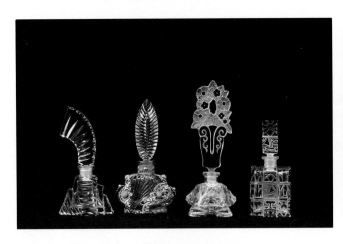

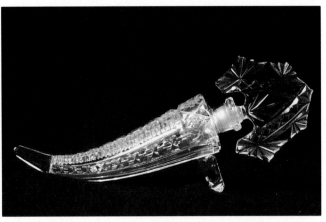

97. Clear/pink, 5-1/4".
98. Pink, jeweled filigree, 5-1/2".
99. Clear and frosted, 6-1/2".
100. Clear and frosted, 4-5/8".

101. Clear, horn-shaped bottle, hard to find, 8-1/2" long.

104. Clear/blue, sunbonnet lady, scarce, 6".
105. Green, flapper dancing, scarce, 5".
106. Blue, Little Bo Peep, scarce, 5-3/4".

102. Turquoise, rare, 7-3/8".

103. Clear and frosted, butterfly among flowers/ red, rare, 6-1/2".

107. Clear/pink, 6-1/4".
108. Green, 5".

109. Blue, 4-1/2".
110. Blue, 7-1/4".
111. Blue, silver decoration, oriental man playing flute, 4-1/2".

112. Purple, 5-1/2".
113. Purple, 7-3/8".
114. Purple, 5-1/2".

115. Heather, rare, 5".
116. Clear and frosted/heather, rare, 6".

117. Purple, 5".
118. Clear and frosted/purple, 4-3/4".
119. Purple, 3-5/8".

120. Purple, 5".
121. Purple, 5-1/4".
122. Purple, 5-1/4".

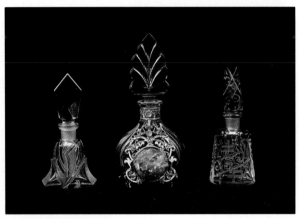

123. Purple, 4-3/4".
124. Purple, 5-3/4".

125. Purple, 4-1/4".
126. Purple, jeweled filigree, 5-3/4".
127. Purple, 4-1/2".

129 (Far left). Clear and frosted, Renaissance troubadour wearing a cape is playing a lute, 5-1/2".

130 (Left). Clear and frosted, oriental landscape, 7-1/8".

128. Clear and frosted, butterfly stopper, 4-1/4".

131. Clear and frosted, 18th-century couple sitting on grass holding hands, 5-3/4".

132. Clear and frosted, 18th-century couple, lady holding fan, gentleman holding a bouquet, 7-1/4".

133. Clear and frosted, two cranes, 7-1/4".

134. Clear and frosted, bird of paradise, 5-3/4".

135. Clear and frosted, two faces, 5-1/4".

136. Clear and frosted, 6-1/2".
137. Clear and frosted, 7".
138. Clear and frosted, 6-1/2".

139. Clear and frosted, 5-3/4".
140. Clear and frosted, 6-1/2".
141. Clear and frosted, 5-7/8".

142. Clear, 6".
143. Clear and frosted, 4-7/8".
144. Clear, 6".

145. Blue/clear, 7-1/2".
146. Clear, 8-1/2".
147. Clear, 7-1/2".

148. Clear, 10-1/2". Possible mismatch.

149 (Far left). Purple (extremely light coloration), fine engraved flower decoration, extra-long dauber, 7-1/8".

150 (Left). Clear and frosted, tree holding two birds and nest/purple, 9".

151. Clear and frosted, 3-1/2".
152. Blue, 4-3/4".
153. Clear, 3-1/2".

154. Blue, 5-1/2".
155. Blue/clear, 5-1/4".
156. Clear/Blue, 5-1/4".

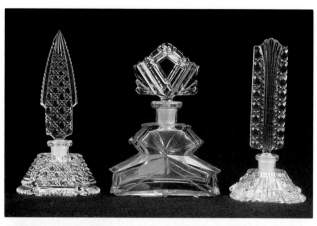

157. Clear, 6".
158. Blue, 5-1/2".
159. Clear, 5-7/8".

160. Clear/heather, rare, 5-3/4".
161. Clear/heather, rare, 6".
162. Clear/heather, rare, 5-7/8".

163. Blue, pair of love birds/clear, 4-7/8".

164. Clear and frosted, leaping ballerina with three butterflies/pink, 6-1/2".

165. Pink, sitting nude with a bow in one hand has cupid standing next to her, 4-3/4".

166. Clear and frosted, woman holding a flower-filled cornucopia is standing on a butterfly/pink, 6-3/4".

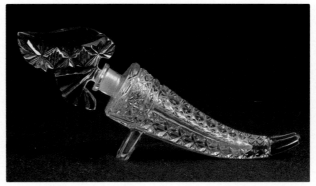

169. Blue, horn-shaped bottle, hard to find, 8-3/4".

167. Pink/clear and pink, two-piece bottle, 6".

168. Blue/clear, two-piece bottle, 6-1/4".

170. Clear and frosted/pink, 9-3/4".

172. Pink, engraved flowers, 5-1/4".

171. Clear and frosted/pink, 10-1/2".

173. Clear/blue, 6-1/2".

174. Blue, 7-1/2".
175. Clear and frosted, peacock/blue, 7-1/2".
176. Blue, 7-1/2".

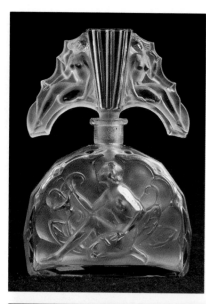

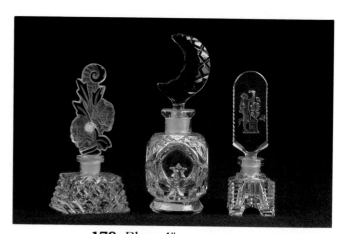

177. Frosted pink, two nudes on stopper, molded nude touching a flower on bottle, 6-1/8".

178. Blue, 4".
179. Blue, 5".
180. Blue, nude with knee on pedestal, 4".

181. Clear and frosted/blue, 6-1/8".
182. Clear and frosted/blue, 4-7/8".
183. Clear and frosted, nude standing on ball/blue, 5-1/2".

184. Blue, 5".
185. Blue, 6-1/2".
186. Blue/clear, 5-1/2".

187. Pink, 6-1/4".
188. Pink/clear, 6".
189. Pink, 6-1/4".

190. Pink, 5-7/8".
191. Pink, 7-7/8".
192. Pink, 6-3/4".

193. Pink, 6-1/4".
194. Pink, 6".
195. Pink, 6-1/8".
196. Pink, 6-1/2".

197. Blue, 5-3/4".
198. Blue, 6-1/8".
199. Blue, 5-7/8".

200 (Far left). Clear and frosted, molded flower design/opaque red, molded bird, rare, mismatched bottle and stopper, 7-1/4".

201 (Left). Opaque blue, two men playing musical instruments on stopper, rare, 7-1/2".

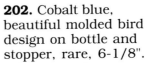

202. Cobalt blue, beautiful molded bird design on bottle and stopper, rare, 6-1/8".

203. Opaque green molded deco nude woman on bottle, 7-3/4".

204. Amberina, very rare/clear, 7-3/4".

205. Clear/opaque black, nude butterfly woman, possible mismatched bottle and stopper, 8".

206. Amberina, very rare, pressed glass, 5-1/4".

207. Clear and frosted/red, rare, 4-3/8".
208. Clear and frosted/red, rare, 4-1/8".

209. Clear and frosted/yellow, 6".
210. Clear and frosted/vaseline, rare, 6".
211. Clear and frosted/yellow, 5-7/8".

212. Red/clear, 5-1/2".
213. Red/clear, 4-3/8".
214. Red/clear and frosted, 5-1/4".

215. Green, 5-1/2".
216. Green, court jester, 4-1/2".
217. Green, 5-5/8".

218. Clear and frosted, flowers growing from basket, double stopper/green, 7-3/4".

219. Green, daisies/ clear, 9-1/2".

220. Clear and frosted, dancing woman/yellow, 6".

221. Yellow, 8".

222. Clear and frosted, man playing pipes for three dancing women/yellow, 6".

Opaque green, three-piece set: **(223.)** Atomizer, 5-3/4"; **(224.)** Powder box, 2-1/2"; **(225.)** Bottle, 6".

Blue, very rare complete matching dresser set: **(226.)** Bottles, 6"; **(227.)** Powder box, 2"; **(228.)** Mirror tray, 19" long.

229. Clear and frosted, lady dressed in an ornate late 18th-century gown with panniers and low-cut bodice/yellow, 7".

230. Clear and frosted, ballerina holding her arms above her head, 5-5/8".

231. Yellow, large prism stopper, 9-1/2".

232. Red/clear, 4".
233. Red/clear, 3-1/4".
234. Red/clear, 4".

235. Red, dancer holding garland/clear, 3-3/4".
236. Red/clear, 5-1/2".
237. Red/clear, 3-1/2".

238. Red/clear, 6-1/4".
239. Red/clear, 5-1/4".
240. Red/clear, 5-1/2".

Clear, three-piece set: **(241.)** painted decoration bottles, 4"; **(242.)** powder, 2".

243. Green, 6-1/4".
244. Green/clear, 5-1/4".
245. Clear/green, 6-1/2".

246. Green, 4-1/2".
247. Clear/green, jeweled filigree, 5-1/4".
248. Green, 4-3/4".

249. Yellow, 5".
250. Yellow, regency couple, 5".
251. Yellow, 4-1/4".

252. Clear and frosted, flower pot/amber, 6-3/4".

253. Yellow, 6-1/4".
254. Clear and frosted/yellow, 7-3/4".
255. Clear and frosted/yellow, 6-1/2".

256. Green, 3-3/4".
257. Green/clear, 4".
258. Green, 5".

259. Purple/clear, 4-7/8".
260. Clear/yellow, 3-3/4".
261. Purple, 4-1/4".

262. Blue, lady wearing a straw poke bonnet enhanced with ribbons and flowers is enclosed by a decorative ribbon of glass, 8-1/2".

263. Marigold flash, 4-1/2".
264. Clear, engraved design, gold trim, 5-1/2".
265. Clear and frosted, atomizer, 4-3/4".

42

266. Green/clear, 5-3/4".
267. Clear, three-lens stopper/green, 5".
268. Green/clear, 4-3/4".

269. Yellow/clear, 4".
270. Clear, 4-1/2".
271. Yellow, 5".

272, 273. Two bottles decorated with trapped air bubbles, 4" and 2-1/4".

274. Clear, 7-1/2".
275. Clear and frosted, double stopper, 6".

276. Teal blue, rare/clear, 5".

277. Milk glass, gold decoration, 6".
278. Frosted blue satin glass, 6-3/4".

279. Blue, 4-3/4".
280. Blue, 4-3/4".
281. Cobalt blue, rare, 5".

282. Clear and frosted, 3-3/4".
283. Blue, 4".
284. Blue/clear, 4-1/4".

285. Blue, 7".
286. Clear/blue, 6-3/4".
287. Blue, jeweled filigree, 7".

288. Blue, 6-1/4".
289. Blue/clear, 6".
290. Blue, 6-3/4".

291. Blue, fairy with flowers, 5-1/4".
292. Clear and frosted/blue, 6-3/4".
293. Blue, 5-1/4".

294. Blue, jeweled filigree, 3-3/4".
295. Blue/clear, 4-1/4".
296. Clear and frosted/blue, 3-3/4".

297. Clear, 5-3/4".
298. Blue/clear, 4-1/4".
299. Clear, 5-1/4".

300 (Far left). Clear and frosted, nude child presenting flowers to a Grecian lady, 5".

301 (Left). Frosted turquoise, rare, fan stopper, molded detailed ladies' faces on sides of bottle, 6-1/4".

302. Gray, three Dutch children wearing traditional clothing including wooden shoes/clear, 5".

303 (Far Left). Clear and frosted, lady carrying baskets trailing flowers under each arm/purple, 6-3/4".

304 (Left). Clear and frosted, 18th-century couple (called George and Martha Washington by many) surrounded by a circle of roses/blue, 7".

305. Clear and frosted, framed cameo-like portrait of a lady with hair in ringlets, 7-1/2".

306 (Far Left). Clear and frosted, flower-basket stopper, 8-1/4".

307 (Left). Blue, draped nude with arms uplifted standing under an arch of flowers, 8-3/4".

308. Clear and frosted, 18th-century beauty standing before her dressing table and mirror, broken neck on bottle, 8-1/4".

309. Clear and frosted, Diana the Huntress holding her traditional bow is petting a deer, double stopper, 7-1/4".

310. Clear and frosted, 18th-century lady in fancy dress holds fan near her face, 8-1/2".

311. Clear and frosted, pair of 18th-century lovers sitting on a rococo bench, 6".

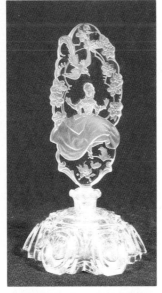

312 (Far left). Clear and frosted, Gibson Girl from the Gay Nineties holding a bouquet in one hand and her hat in the other, 8".

313 (Left). Clear and frosted, yellow staining, traipsing lady in a very full skirt is surrounded by flowers and one bird, 9-3/4".

314. Yellow, basket of flowers, 7-3/4".

315 (Far left). Clear and frosted/yellow, 10-3/4".

316 (Left). Green, roses on stopper, kneeling woman with extended arms on bottle, scarce, 5-3/4".

317. Clear and frosted, woman with windblown skirt is leaning against a stalk of flowers/yellow, 6-3/4".

318. Frosted green, molded roses on stopper and bottle, no marks, 5-3/4".

319. Clear, 5-7/8".
320. Pink, 6".
321. Clear, 6-1/4".

322. Pink, 4-1/2".
323. Pink, 5-1/2".
324. Pink, 4-1/2".

325. Clear, 6".
326. Blue, 5-3/4".
327. Clear, prism stopper, jeweled filigree, 5-1/2".

328. Purple, 6".
329. Purple, 5-3/4".
330. Purple, 6".

331. Blue/clear, bell-shaped bottle, 5-1/2".

332. Pink, 7-1/4".
333. Clear/pink, 6-1/2".
334. Pink, 6-1/2".

335. Clear/pink, 7".
336. Pink, Egyptian-motif jeweled filigree, 6-1/4".
337. Pink, metal filigree, 6-1/4".

338. Clear and frosted, 6-1/2".
339. Clear and frosted/pink, pressed glass, 7-1/4".
340. Clear and frosted, 7".

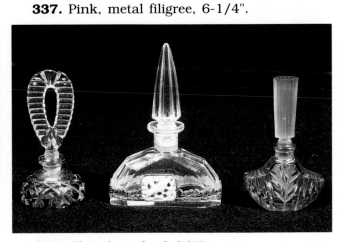

341. Clear/purple, 3-3/4".
342. Clear, jeweled filigree, pressed glass, 4-1/2".
343. Purple, 3-3/4".

344. Pink, 6-1/4".
345. Clear/pink, 5-3/4".
346. Pink, 5-3/4".

347. Clear and frosted/gray, 6-3/4".
348. Purple, 6-1/2".
349. Clear and frosted/purple, 7".

350. Clear and frosted, 3-1/2".
351. Pink/clear, 3-3/4".
352. Clear and frosted/pink, 3-3/4".

353. Clear/opaque black, jeweled filigree, 5-1/2".
354. Clear, black enameled decoration, 5-3/4".
355. Clear/opaque, black, jeweled filigree, 6-1/4".

356. Clear and frosted, 7-3/4".
357. Clear, paperweight bottle, 7-3/4".

358. Opaque black/clear and frosted, 5-3/4".
359. Opaque black/cased blue, silver decoration, 4".
360. Clear/opaque black, 4-1/2".

361 (Far left). Clear and frosted, curious goose watches a posturing nude with scarf/pink, 5-3/4".

362 (Left). Clear and frosted, nude woman twirling her hair is posed in a fountain/ pink, 7-1/4".

363. Clear and frosted, six arches enclose a bird and flowers/pink 7".

364. Clear and frosted, thoughtful nude woman framed by a simple arch/pink, 7-1/4".

365. Clear and frosted, pink staining, side view of a leaping nude sporting stylized butterfly wings and antenna/pink, 8-1/2".

366. Clear and frosted, man in bell-bottom trousers and woman in a short skirt are dancing the jitterbug, double stopper/blue, 7-1/2".

367 (Far left). Blue, bottle shaped like woman dressed in fancy hoop skirt, the head forms the stopper, 6".

368 (Left). Blue, willowy nude dances with scarves against a background of curlicues, 6".

369. Clear and frosted, lady sitting on a baluster admires a peacock perched in a flowering tree/blue, 8-1/4".

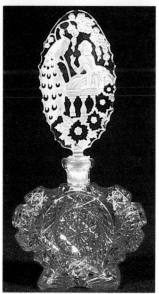

370 (Far left). Clear and frosted, woman wearing a long dress with ruffled hem is standing on a giant daisy/blue, 8".

371 (Left). Clear and frosted, two birds with touching wings and beaks/blue, 8".

372. Clear and frosted, nude wood nymph with slender wings is smelling a flower/pink, 6-3/4".

373. Blue, unusual asymmetric cut stopper, 5-1/2".

374. Opalescent, very rare, molded rose design, 4-1/8".

Clear, two-piece crystal set: **(375.)** Well-done enamel decoration box, 2-3/4"; **(376.)** Bottle, 7-1/4".

377. Blue, jeweled filigree, 9-1/4".

378 (Right). Green opaque, simple molded flower design, 6-1/4".

379 (Far right). Frosted pink, frosted white three-dimensional bird set in metal filigree is perched on the hoop-shaped stopper, very unusual, minor damage, 6".

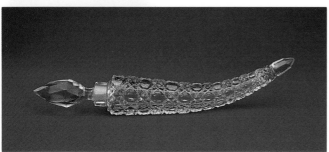

380. Yellow, horn-shaped lay-down bottle, 9" long.

381 (Right). Red, cut to clear bottle and stopper, 5-1/4".

382 (Far right). Gray, nude woman riding a leaping goat is grasping his horns, 5".

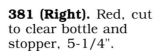

383. Clear/opaque black, jeweled filigree, 8-1/2".
384. Ivory, very rare, two birds touching wings and beaks/opaque black, jeweled filigree, 8".

385. Vaseline, rare, angel holding a vase faces a cupid playing pipes on stopper, molded draped dancers on bottle, 6-3/8".

386. Opaque blue, rare, butterfly on stopper, molded nude woman with very long hair holds a flower garland on bottle, 5".

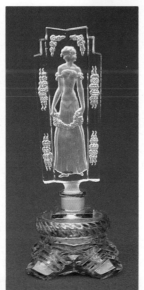

387 (Far left). Clear and frosted, kneeling nude male archer with his bow string pulled ready to fire/green, 5-1/8".

388 (Left). Clear and frosted, woman in long off-the-shoulder gown holds a garland of flowers in her hands/green, 6-1/2".

389. Clear and frosted, little boy is blowing a man-in-moon shaped bubble towards two birds perched on a wash-tub/green, 5-1/2".

390 (Far left). Green, lady in a tiered skirt is shaking a flowering tree, 6-1/2".

391 (Left). Clear and frosted, small bird hovering over a flowering plant, 5".

392. Clear and frosted, lady wearing a hoop skirt standing before a large wreath of flowers, 5-3/4".

52

393. Clear and frosted, woman shading her eyes with one hand holds a flowering branch in the other, 5-1/2".

394. Clear and frosted, chic lady wearing long dress and wide-brimmed hat holds bouquet and has a dog laying at her feet, 9-3/8".

395. Pink, Pan the goat boy (Greek god of pastures and flocks) holds a harp on one shaggy knee/clear, 4-1/2".

396. Pink, woman wearing long dress is carrying large flat basket of flowers on her shoulder/clear, 6-1/4".

397 (Right). Clear and frosted, attractive kneeling nude with three large chrysanthemums/pink, 6".

398 (Far right). Clear and frosted, portrait of genteel 18th-century lady wearing large hat decorated with plumes/purple, jeweled filigree, 5-1/4".

399 (Far left). Clear and frosted, maiden wearing laced-up dirndl dress sits among roses/blue, molded cupid design, 8".

400 (Left). Clear and frosted, double stopper, lady circus performer and large jungle cat are balancing on a big ball/pink, 7".

401 (Far right). Clear and frosted, harem dancer in diaphanous pants is holding a tambourine/pink, 6-1/8.

402 (Far left). Clear and frosted, lady playing a tambourine is clad in transparent gown/pink, 7-3/8".

403 (Left). Clear and frosted, 18th-century lovers, sitting under a flowering tree on a bench, have two sheep at their feet/pink, 8-1/2".

404. Clear and frosted, lady wearing long dress with ruffled hem has bouquet in her arm and flowers at her feet/blue, jeweled filigree, 7".

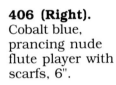

406 (Right). Cobalt blue, prancing nude flute player with scarfs, 6".

407 (Far right). Cranberry, graduated color from clear to red, 5-1/2".

405. Clear and frosted, double stopper, man with cane and woman in fancy ball gown/pink, 7-1/4".

408. Opaque red, rare, molded deco design of leaves and circles, 6-1/2".

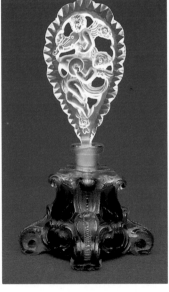

409. Clear and frosted, two angels playing the violin and cymbals/brown, rare, 7-3/4".

Cranberry opalescent, mold-blown hobnail design three-piece dresser set:
(410.) bottles, 5-1/4"; **(411.)** box, 4".

412. Clear and frosted/purple, 5-1/8".
413. Purple, very rare bead dauber, 5-3/4".
414. Purple, screw top, 3-7/8".

Green, three-piece vanity set:
(415.) bottles, 5"; **(416.)** box, 2".

417. Amber, 6".
418. Clear/opaque green, jeweled filigree, 5-1/2".
419. Amber, 6".

420. Clear, 9-1/2".

421. Yellow, 8-3/4".

Blue, three-piece vanity set: **(422.)** Bottles, 5"; **(423.)** Box, 2".

424. Blue, 4".
425. Pink, pressed glass, 5-1/4".
426. Blue, 7-1/8".
427. Pink, 3-5/8".

428. Clear and frosted/gray, 5-1/2".
429. Opaque black/clear, 7-1/2".
430. Clear/gray, 4-1/2".

Red/green, crackle finish, pressed glass, three-piece dresser set: **(431.)** Bottles, 7-1/2"; **(432.)** Powder box, 4-1/2".

433. Amber, 3-1/4".
434. Amber, 6-1/2".
435. Amber, 6-1/2".
436. Amber, pressed glass, jeweled filigree, 3-1/2".

437. Green, 4-3/8".
438. Green, 4-1/2".
439. Green, 4-3/4".

440. Green, 5-3/8".
441. Metal stopper, clear pressed glass, jeweled filigree, 5".
442. Green, 7".

443. Green, jeweled filigree, 4-1/8".
444. Green, atomizer, jeweled filigree, 3-7/8".
445. Green, jeweled filigree, 4-1/2".

446. Green, 5-1/4".
447. Green, two fairies on a rose/clear, 7-1/4".
448. Green, 5-1/8".

449. Green, jeweled filigree, 4-1/2".
450. Green, arrow/clear, 5".
451. Green, 4-1/2".

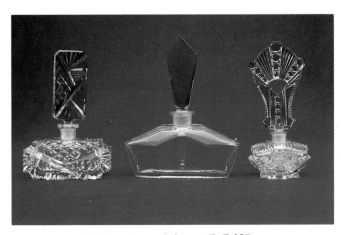

452. Green/clear, 5-5/8".
453. Green/clear, 6".
454. Green/clear, 6".

455. Green/clear and green, two-piece bottle, 5-1/2".
456. Green, jeweled filigree, 5-3/4".
457. Green/clear to green, two-piece bottle, 5-3/4".

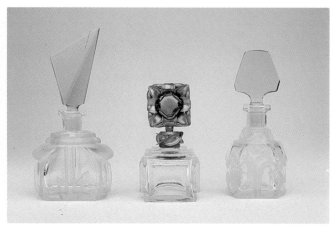

458. Red/clear, 3-1/4".
459. Metal stopper with jewels/clear, pressed glass, jeweled filigree, 4-3/4".
460. Red/clear, 4-1/2".

461. Purple/clear and frosted, 6".
462. Metal stopper with jewel/clear, pressed glass, 4".
463. Purple/clear and frosted, 6".

464. Clear and frosted, 4-3/4".
465. Clear, 2-1/4".
466. Clear and frosted, 4-3/4".

467. Clear, 6-1/4".
468. Clear, 5-1/2".
469. Clear, 6-1/4".

470. Clear and frosted, 6-1/2".
471. Clear, 6-1/2".
472. Clear, 6-1/4".

473. Clear, 5-3/4".
474. Clear and frosted, 7-1/2".
475. Clear, 5-1/2".

476. Clear and frosted, 5-1/4".
477. Clear and frosted, minor damage, 6-1/8".
478. Clear and frosted, 5".

479. Clear, unusual design, 6-5/8".
480. Clear, unusual design, 5-1/8".

481. Clear and frosted, 7-1/4".
482. Clear, 10".
483. Clear and frosted, 7-1/2".

484. Clear and frosted, 7".
485. Clear and frosted, 7-1/2".
486. Clear and frosted, 7-1/2".

487. Clear, 5-1/8".
488. Clear and frosted, 5".
489. Clear, 5-1/8".

490. Yellow/clear, 4".
491. Clear, 2-3/4".
492. Clear, 3-1/2".

493. Clear and frosted, 6-1/8".
494. Clear, black enameling, 7".
495. Clear and frosted, 5-3/4".

496. Clear and frosted, 6-1/4".
497. Clear and frosted, 6-3/4".
498. Clear and frosted, 5-1/2".

499. Clear and frosted, 7".
500. Clear, 5-3/4".
501. Clear, 7".

502. Clear and frosted, 5-1/2".
503. Clear and frosted, 8".
504. Clear and frosted, 6".

505. Yellow, 5-1/4".
506. Yellow, 6-1/2".
507. Vaseline, 5-1/2".

508. Yellow, 7".
509. Yellow/clear, 5-3/4".
510. Amber, prism stopper/clear, 6-1/2".

511. Yellow/clear, 5-3/8".
512. Yellow, 5".
513. Yellow/clear, 6".

514. Yellow, 6-3/4".
515. Yellow/clear, 6-7/8".
516. Yellow, 6-1/2".

517. Amber, 5-1/2".
518. Amber, filigree, cupid decoration, 6-1/2".
519. Amber, initial, 5-1/4".

520. Pink/clear, 3-1/2".
521. Clear/pink, 5-1/2".
522. Clear and frosted/pink, 3-3/8".

523. Pink, 4-1/2".
524. Pink, 6-1/2".
525. Pink, 4-1/2".

526. Pink, 5-5/8".
527. Pink, 8-1/4".
528. Pink, 6".

529. Clear and frosted, lady with dog/pink, 4-7/8".

530. Pink/clear, 5-3/4".

531. Pink, kneeling woman holding vines, 4-3/4".

532. Pink/clear, 6".

533. Pink, woman blowing bubbles at cupid, jeweled filigree, 5".

534. Pink/clear, 5-3/4".

535. Blue, lovebirds/clear, 4-3/4".

536. Clear and frosted/blue, 6-1/2".

537. Blue/clear, 4-1/2".

538. Blue/clear, 6".

539. Blue/clear and blue, two-piece bottle, 6".

540. Blue, curved stopper/clear, 6".

541. Blue, jeweled filigree, 3-3/4".

542. Blue, 5-3/4".

543. Blue, 4-1/8".

544. Blue, 6".

545. Blue, 6-3/4".

546. Blue, 6".

547. Blue/clear, 6".
548. Blue/clear, 7-1/4".
549. Blue/clear, 5-3/4".

550. Blue, 5-3/4".
551. Blue, 6-1/2".
552. Blue/clear, 5-3/4".

553. Blue, 4-3/4".
554. Blue, applied glass flowers, 4-1/2".
555. Blue, metal filigree, 5".

556. Blue/clear, 8-1/2".
557. Blue/clear, 7".
558. Blue/clear, 8".

559. Pink, jeweled filigree, 5-1/2".
560. Pink, 8".
561. Pink, jeweled filigree, 7".

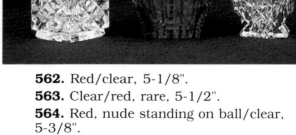

562. Red/clear, 5-1/8".
563. Clear/red, rare, 5-1/2".
564. Red, nude standing on ball/clear, 5-3/8".

565. Gray, 4-7/8".
566. Gray, jeweled filigree, 4-3/4".
567. Gray, 5-3/4".

568. Clear/opaque black, jeweled filigree, 4-1/2". **569.** Clear/opaque black, jeweled filigree butterfly, 5-1/2". **570.** Clear/opaque black, jeweled filigree, 4-1/4".

571. Opaque black/clear, opaque blackbase, 5".
572. Opaque black/clear, 4-5/8".
573. Opaque black/clear and frosted, 5-5/8".

574. Clear and frosted, graceful ballerina standing on her toes is wearing a flounced skirt/pink, 6-1/8".

575. Clear and frosted, butterfly woman with delicate wings is clad in a short dress/pink, 6".

576 (Far left). Clear and frosted, flapper bathing beauty/blue, 6".

577 (Left). Clear and frosted, sensual nude identical twins strike matching poses/pink, 10".

578. Blue, decorative ribbon of glass frames a short-haired woman holding flowers, 8".

579. Clear and frosted, double stopper, three nude females pose with their knees touching/ blue, 7".

580. Clear and frosted, galloping horses with flowing manes are ridden by a single nude woman/pink, 6-1/2".

581. Clear and frosted, two bare-footed women dancing together, one in a strapless gown, the other in Egyptian costume, 6-1/2".

582. Clear and frosted, peacock surrounded by climbing ivy, 6-1/2".

583 (Right). Clear and frosted, double stopper, nude female holding a ball plays with a Russian wolfhound, 7-1/2".

584 (Far right). Clear and frosted, 18th-century lovers with canine audience reenact the balcony scene from "Romeo and Juliet," 7-3/4".

585 (Far left). Clear and frosted, man and woman dance-team doing the tango on a horseshoe-shaped ribbon of glass, 6".

586 (Left). Clear and frosted, double stopper, two nude women running and holding onto one very long scarf, 10".

587. Clear and frosted, man wearing a double-breasted cutaway coat and cravat has arm around lady holding a bouquet/yellow, jeweled filigree, 7".

588 (Far left). Opaque turquoise, very rare, molded lily-of-the-valley design on the stopper and bottle, 7".

589 (Left). Opaque green, three-dimensional mask design/opaque black, 6".

590. Clear and frosted, pair of three-dimensional nudes hold a bottle between their hands and knees, filigree, porcelain medallion, no marks, 6".

591. Clear and frosted, 18th-century couple holding hands/red, rare, 4-3/4".

592. Clear and frosted, very unusual three-dimensional horizontal nude/opaque black, 3-1/8".

593. Opaque green, molded man with bow, in a loin-cloth or short skirt, aiming at flock of birds, 3-3/4".

594 (Far left). Opaque orange, very rare, flying birds on stopper, pair of deco nudes on bottle, 5".

595 (Left). Clear and frosted, roses/red, rare, 9-1/4".

596. Amber, molded multi-flower and leaf design in frosted finish with ground transparent amber leaping deer on front, molded decoration continued on bottom of bottle is extremely rare, large molded single-flower stopper, 7".

PURSE, DRAM AND MINI BOTTLES

Dram or mini bottles. **597.** Pink/clear, 3-1/2". **598.** Blue, 4". **599.** Pink/clear, 4". **600.** Pink, 3-1/2". **601.** Purple, jeweled filigree, 3-1/2". **602.** Pink/clear, 3".

Dram or mini bottles. **603.** Clear/opaque black, 3". **604.** Clear/opaque black, jeweled filigree, 2-3/4". **605.** Red/clear, 3-1/4". **606.** Purple, 4". **607.** Red/clear, 3-1/2". **608.** Clear/opaque black, 2-3/4". **609.** Clear/opaque black, 2-7/8".

Dram or mini bottles. **610.** Green/clear, 2-3/4". **611.** Clear and frosted/blue, 3-1/2". **612.** Green/clear, 3-3/4". **613.** Blue/clear, 4". **614.** Green, 3-1/4". **615.** Blue, 4". **616.** Green/clear, jeweled filigree, 2-1/4".

Dram or mini bottles. **617.** Yellow, 3-1/4". **618.** Yellow/clear, 2-1/4". **619.** Yellow, 3-3/4". **620.** Yellow, 2-5/8". **621.** Yellow, 3".

Dram and mini bottles. **622.** Clear, 2-3/4". **623.** Clear, 2-7/8". **624.** Clear and frosted, girl holding hoop overhead, 3-1/2". **625.** Clear and frosted, 3".

Perfumettes.
626. Pink, 2-1/8".
627. Pink, 2-1/4".
628. Pink, 2-1/8".

629, 630, 631, 632. Purse bottles, jeweled filigree, 1-1/2" to 3".

633, 634, 635, 636. Purse bottles, jeweled filigree, 2-1/4" to 3".

637, 638, 639, 640, 641. Purse bottles, jeweled filigree, 2" to 3".

Dram or mini bottles.
642. Red/opaque black, 2-3/4". **643.** Red/clear, 2-3/4". **644.** Clear/opaque black, jeweled filigree, 3-1/2".

645, 646, 647. Three dram bottles with fox or dog shaped stoppers, two are 2-3/4", one is 2-1/4".

Perfumettes. **648.** Green/clear, 2-1/4". **649.** Clear/green, 2-1/8". **650.** Red/clear, 2-3/8". **651.** Blue, 2-1/8". **652.** Pink/clear, 2-1/4".

Dram or mini bottles. **653.** Red and white glass flowers/clear, 2". **654.** Red/clear, 3-1/2". **655.** Red, heart/clear, 2". **656.** Red/clear and frosted, 1-3/8".

657. Clear and frosted, woman's head/opaque black, 3". **658.** Clear/purple, 1-1/8". **659.** Teal green, very rare/clear, 2-1/2".

Dram or mini bottles. **660.** Jeweled metal stopper/clear, 3-3/8". **661.** Blue, 4". **662.** Blue, cupid with bow/clear and frosted, filigree, 3-1/2". **663.** Blue/clear, jeweled filigree, 3-7/8". **664.** Clear/blue, 3-1/2".

665, 666, 667, 668, 669. Purse bottles, jeweled filigree, 1-3/8" to 2-1/2".

670, 671, 672, 673, 674. Dram bottles, jeweled top, screw top, average height 2-1/2".

675, 676, 677, 678, 679, 680. Dram bottles, jeweled tops with lucky charms attached by chain, screw top, average height 2-1/2".

Dram or mini bottles. **681.** Clear/purple, jeweled filigree, 4". **682.** Clear, 2-1/8". **683.** Clear, 4-1/2". **684.** Yellow, 2-3/4". **685.** Purple, 2-3/4". **686.** Blue/clear, 4-1/4". **687.** Pink/clear, 4".

Dram or mini bottles. **688.** Clear to frosted, 3-1/2". **689.** Green/clear, 4". **690.** Clear and frosted, 3-3/4". **691.** Green/clear, 3-5/8". **692.** Clear and frosted, 3-3/8".

693, 694, 695. Purse bottles, jeweled filigree, 1-7/8" to 2-1/4".

696, 697, 698. Three opaque glass purse bottles with molded decoration, screw tops, 2-1/8" to 2-3/4".

TWIN SETS

699. Purple/clear twin set, 2-1/4", with **700.** Purple tray.

701 (Far left). Red/clear twin set, 3", with **702.** Red tray.

703 (Left). Cobalt blue/clear twin set, 4-1/8", **704.** Cobalt tray.

ATOMIZERS

705. Green, atomizer, 3-5/8".
706. Green, atomizer, 3".
707. Green, atomizer, 3".

708. Amber, atomizer, 3-1/4".
709. Amber, atomizer, 6-1/2".

710. Clear, atomizer, enameled decoration, 7-3/4". **711.** Clear and orange, bottle, gold decoration, jeweled metalwork, 8-1/2". **712.** Mottled colors, atomizer, 7".

713. Clear and frosted, atomizer, enameled flower design, 6-1/2". **714.** Purple, atomizer, gold decoration, 7". **715.** Blue, atomizer, luster finish, enameled roses, 6-1/2". **716.** Mottled colors, atomizer, satin finish, 6-1/2".

717. Cobalt blue, atomizer, gold decoration, 7-1/4". **718.** Cobalt blue, atomizer, clear jewel, enameled decoration, 8-1/4". **719.** Cobalt blue, atomizer, blue jewel, enameled decoration, 7-3/8".

720. Red, black base, atomizer, 6-1/2". **721.** Black, atomizer, gold decoration, 9-1/2". **722.** Green, cased glass, atomizer, applied black glass decoration, 8".

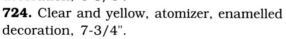

723. Clear and frosted, atomizer, enamelled decoration, 6-3/4". **724.** Clear and yellow, atomizer, enamelled decoration, 7-3/4".

725. Blue, atomizer, 2-7/8". **726.** Clear/pink, atomizer, 3-3/4". **727.** Blue, atomizer, 3-1/4".

BOUDOIR ACCESSORIES

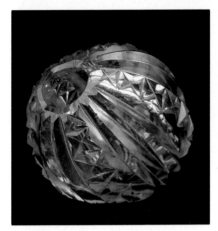

728. Blue, cotton holder, 2-1/2".

729. Yellow, powder box, 2".

730. Purple, powder box, 2-1/4".

731. Green tray, five birds sitting on branch, no marks, 10" long.

732. Green, powder box, 3-1/4".

733. Blue, powder box, pressed glass, 3-1/2".

734. Blue, magnifying mirror, 3".
735. Blue, clock, 2-3/4".
736. Blue, ash or pin tray, 1-1/2".

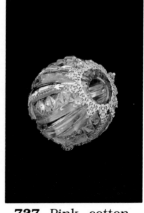

737. Pink, cotton holder, jeweled filigree, 2-3/4".

738. Mottled colors, powder box, metal top with jewel trim, 3".

739, 740, 741, 742, 743. Purse bottles, jeweled filigree, 2" to 3".

Two boxes and one bottle with the same pattern: **(744.)** Small box, 1-1/8"; **(745.)** bottle, 3-3/4"; **(746.)** Large box, 1-3/8".

747. Pink, cotton holder, 2-1/2.

748. Yellow, jeweled filigree, solid perfume container, 1-3/4".

749. Porcelain trinket or powder box with glass top, 2-3/4".

750. Yellow, powder box, 2-1/8".

751. Clear/green, powder box, 2-3/4".

752. Green, powder box, jeweled filigree, 3".

753. Clear and frosted, powder box, enamel decoration, 3-3/4".

754. Blue, powder box, 4-1/2".

755. Pink/clear, powder box, 4".

756. Frosted pink, powder box, pressed glass, 3-1/4".

757. Clear, container, glass screw top, no marks, 2-1/4".

758. Vaseline, the nude figural dauber is extremely rare/clear, jeweled filigree stand, 5".

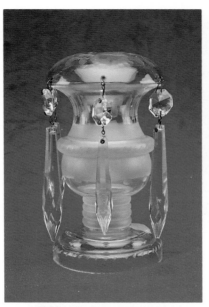

760. Amber, cut to clear, powder box, black enamel decoration, 2".

761. Beautiful and extremely rare hand mirror (unfortunately the handle is missing), 4-3/4".

759. Clear and frosted, perfume lamp with the original cut-crystal prisms, 5-1/4".

763. Magnifying mirror with cut-crystal handle, 6-1/2".

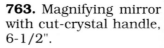

762. Blue, boudoir clock, 3".

765. Blue, pressed glass, satin finish, cotton holder, originally sold for 29 cents, 2-3/8".

764. Pink, talcum-powder shaker, 4-3/4".

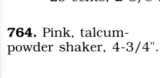

766. Blue, powder box, 2-1/4".

767. Blue, powder box, 2-5/8".

768. Blue, powder box, 3-3/4".

769. Pink, powder box, 4-1/2".

770. Clear, powder box, 2".

771. Blue, pin or ash tray, nude woman, 2-3/4".

772. Pink, powder box, 2-1/2".

773, 774, 775, 776, 777. Perfume lamps, 4-1/4" to 6".

778, 779, 780. Clear, pressed glass toilet bottles with enameled decoration for peroxide, Listerine and boric acid, 4-3/4".

781. Brown, powder or trinket box, 2".

782. Amber, powder box, 3-1/2".

783. Amber, ash tray with metal trim, 1-1/2".

784. Blue, sailing ship, salt, 2-3/4"
785. Green, horse and hounds, salt, 2-1/2".
786. Pink, chariot, salt, 2-1/2".
787. Amber, soccer players, salt, 2-1/4".

788. Pink and blue personal ash trays, 2-1/2" across.

789. Frosted, pin tray, filigree with coral jewel, 2".

790. Amber, double salt, jeweled filigree, 6-1/4" across.

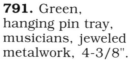

791. Green, hanging pin tray, musicians, jeweled metalwork, 4-3/8".

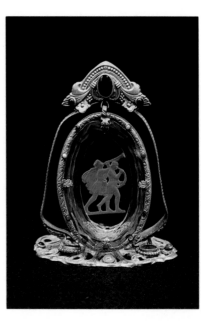

78

792. Opaque black/mottled colors, cased glass, combination perfume bottle and powder box, 7-1/2".

793. Porcelain powder box, 2-3/4".

794. Porcelain powder box, 2".

Red, four-piece toilet set, very rare: **(795.)** Bottles, 6"; **(796.)** Drinking glass, 4"; **(797.)** Covered box, 4".

798. Blue, boudoir clock, 3".

799. Ivory, very rare, cigarette or trinket box, deco nude, 2-1/4".

800. Frosted purple, powder box, molded fish design, nude handle, 6-1/4".

Dresser set. **(801.** Mirror; **802.** Brush)** with jewel and enamel decoration is marked "E & JB." Attributed Czechoslovakia.

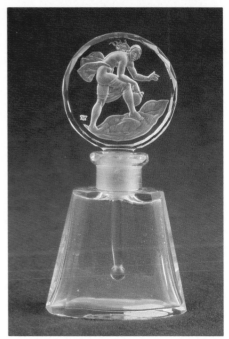

803. Opaque black and frosted, nude Leda with swan, flying swan on stopper, 4".

804. Purple clock, kneeling nude woman blowing bubbles at bird, French clock mechanism, 4".

806, 807. Two frosted glass pin trays with molded nudes, aqua 4-1/2" long, clear 3-1/4" long.

805. Clear and frosted, draped nude holding a water jug is walking uphill, 5".

808. Clear and frosted, semi-nude lady blowing bubbles at cupid on stopper, molded design of cupids, bubbles and birds on bottle, 6-1/2".

809. Turquoise, rare, nude woman blowing bubbles at cupid, 7-1/8".

810. Frosted vase line, rare, nude sitting in seashell stopper, molded fish design on bottle, 6-1/4".

811. Opaque black, toilet bottle, unusual medallion decoration picturing an 18th-century couple, 4-1/2".

812. Clear and frosted, angel playing a triangle, Grecian dancer, boy playing pipes, 4".

813. Opaque black, bird-shaped stopper/clear and frosted, nude woman with headdress touches bird, 4-3/8".

INGRID GLASS

814. Ivory, molded chrysanthemum design bottle and stopper, very rare, 5-1/2.".

815. Pink, lounging nude surrounded by leaves on stopper, grape leaf design on bottle, 7-3/4".

816. Clear and frosted, nude pair of lovers with garland of flowers/green, 5-3/4".

817. Frosted purple, man and woman dancing stopper, molded flower design on bottle, 5-3/4".

JAPANESE COPIES

818. Amber bottle copied from a Czechoslovakian original is marked "made in Japan," 5".

819. Blue and clear Czechoslovakian bottle beside a **(820.)** purple copy made in Japan. Notice the very poor intaglio cutting on the Japanese bottle.

COMMERCIAL BOTTLES

821. Red/clear and frosted, "Triomphe" perfume, 5-1/2". **822.** Clear, "Jeurelle" perfume, 2-1/8". **823.** Clear and frosted, "Jeurelle" perfume, 1-7/8". **824.** Clear and frosted, "Jeurelle" perfume, 2-1/2". **825.** Red/ clear and frosted, "Triomphe" perfume, 4-1/2".

The next eight pages of photographs depict pages from a catalog of opaque green glass, called jade glass, made in Czechoslovakia in the late 1950s. The molds used for this glass-ware were originally made in the 1920s and 1930s.

CONTEMPORARY BOTTLES

826, 827, 828. Examples of the clear and frosted molded glass vanity items produced in Czechoslovakia in the late 1980s.

829. Clear and frosted, flower-basket stopper, molded woman and roses on bottle, circa 1970s, 8".

1

25354/25 cm

25292/18 cm

72/12,5 cm

1006/22 cm

2

25296 10,5 cm

25301 23 cm

25361 18,5 cm

25305/18 cm

82/8 cm

3

25293/23 cm

25303 15 cm

25299/9 cm

25313/16,5 cm

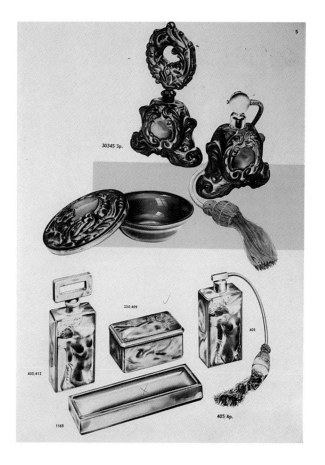

5

30345 3p.

405/413

334/409

405

1165

405/4p.

83

4

1521/9 cm

482/20,5 cm

1166/12,5 cm

361/24 cm

142/80

142

146/147

142/80/3p.

148/15×9 cm

989

467/987

989 990

986

989/4p.

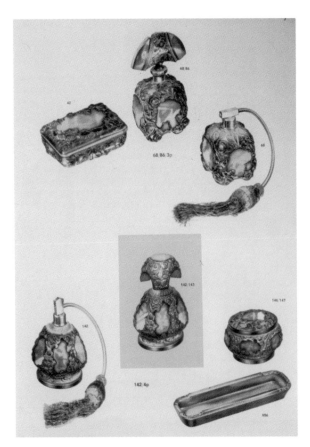

42

68/86

68/86/3p.

68

142/143

146/147

142

142/4p.

986

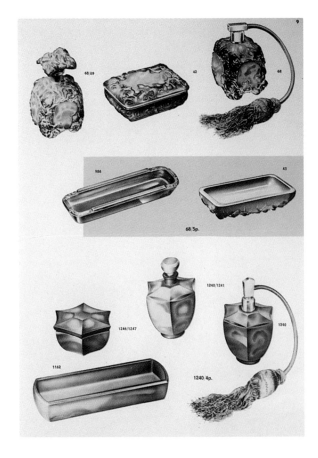

68/89

42

68

986

43

68/5p.

1240/1241

1246/1247

1240

1162

1240/4p.

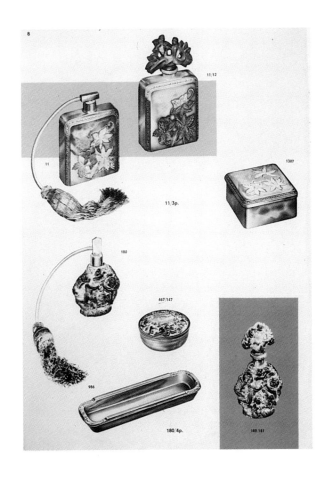

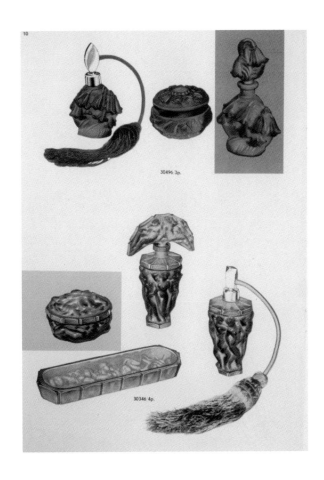

30317/4p.

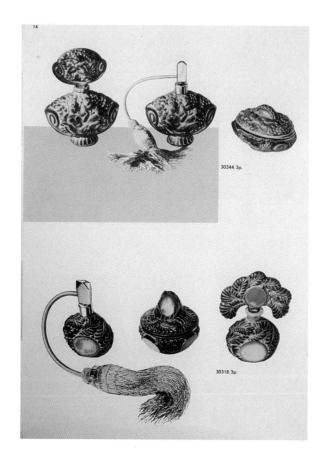

30344/3p.

30318/3p.

30343/3p.

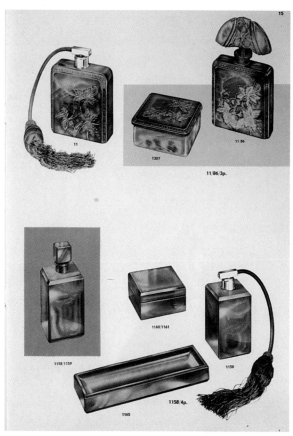

11

1307

11.86

11/86/3p.

1158/1159

1160/1161

1150

1165

1158/4p.

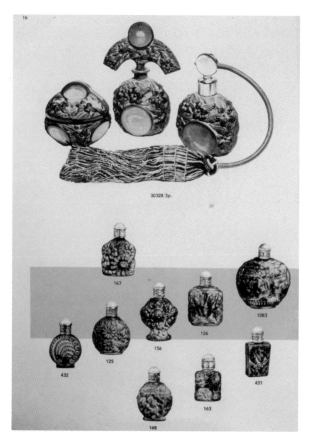

30328/3p.

167

432

125

156

126

1083

168

163

431

17

22594/8 cm

22644/10 cm

13274/14,5 cm

13273/15,5 cm

1264/1265/12,5 cm

86/87/9 cm

19

57/265/12×9 cm

254/11×6,5 cm

227/385/9,5×9 cm

228/6,5 cm

26874/17 cm

106/12,5 cm

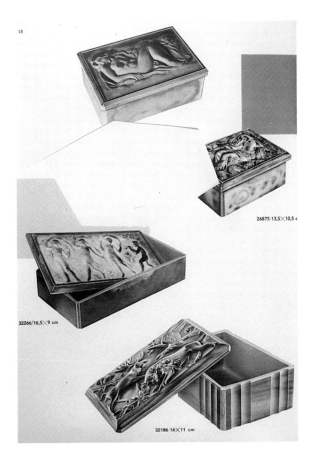

18

26875/13,5×10,5 cm

32266/16,5×9 cm

32186/16×11 cm

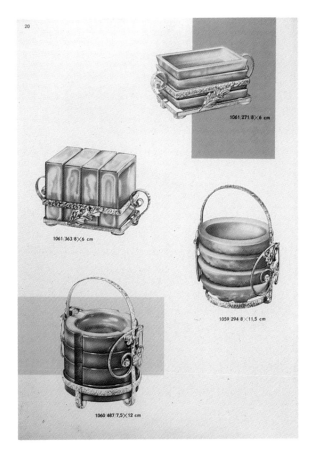

20

1061/271/8×6 cm

1061/363/8×6 cm

1059/294/8×11,5 cm

1060/487/7,5×12 cm

88/17,5 cm

35270/7p.

21998/21 cm

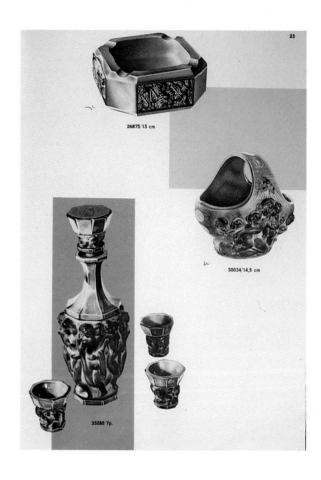

26875/13 cm

50034/14,5 cm

35288/7p.

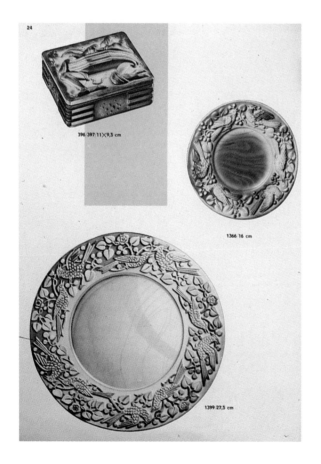

396 397/11×9,5 cm

1366/16 cm

1399/27,5 cm

35290/7p.

32013/22×12 cm

ADVERTISEMENTS

IRVING RICE presents

Art and beauty join hands in the delicacy of these new, sparkling Bohemian glassware toiletries. Crystal bottles with graceful, spire prism tops; facetted with hand cut, hand polished intaglio designs; ground glass stoppers with applicators...Powder and perfume sprays to match, with fool-proof mechanism. Chromium fittings throughout. Silk tubes and long decorative tassels. In new boudoir pastel shades.

1932

THIS IS DEFINITELY A GLASSWARE SEASON

No. 1 retails $1.00
No. 2   "   1.00
No. 3   "   3.00
No. 4   "   2.50
No. 5   "   1.00
No. 6   "   2.00
Others up to $25.00

BOHEMIAN Glassware Toiletries

**ERE IS SMART VARIETY
OR ATTRACTIVE ENSEMBLES**

For the first time complexion mirrors are available with Bohemian crystal handles to harmonize with the perfume bottles and sprays. A choice of over 75 numbers, including Watteau prints and cloisonne backs, with the famous Tells-All magnifying beauty mirror. The long, graceful crystal handles are in intaglio, and duplicate the sparkle and tints of the bottles and jars.

1932

No. 7	retails	$2.00
No. 8	"	1.00
No. 9	"	1.00
No. 10	"	1.50
No. 11	"	1.00
Others up to $5.00		

Genuine Cut Crystal Toiletries by Rice

1933

3. Bohemian cut glass Powder Jar. *Retail* $1.50.

1. Bohemian cut glass Perfume Bottles. *Retail* $1.00 each.

BOHEMIAN CUT CRYSTAL

5. Assortment of six cut glass Bottles in six colors. *Retail* 89c each.

2. Bohemian cut glass Atomizer. *Retail* $1.50. Bottle to match. *Retail* $1.25.

VENETIAN BLOWN GLASS

6. Perfume Bottle and Jar Ensemble. *Retail* $2.00 each piece.

4. Cut glass Bottles filled with Smelling Salts. Three colors. *Retail* $1.50 each.

Irving W. Rice & Co., 15 W. 34th St., N. Y. C.

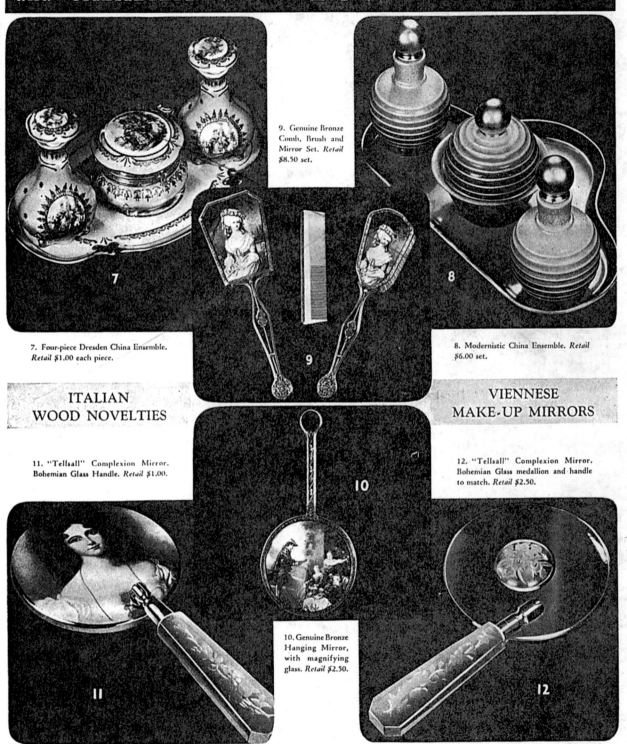

IRVING RICE...

THREE years ago we introduced crystal toiletries for the boudoir. The phenomenal success which stores enjoyed with this merchandise is a matter of record. We predicted large sales at that time and we assure you now that this Fall and Winter you will reach unheard of sales peaks with our new line.

No.	1 — retails		$1.00
No.	2 — "		1.00
No.	3 — "		1.00
No.	4 — "		1.00
No.	5 — "		1.00
No.	6 — "	per set	2.00
No.	7 — "	per set	2.00
No.	8 — "		3.00
No.	9 — "		.50
No.	10 — "		1.00
No.	11 — "		1.00
No.	12 — "		.50
No.	13 — "		.25
No.	14 — "		1.00
No.	15 — "		1.00
No.	16 — "		1.00

FROM all parts of Europe and the Orient we have assembled a huge assortment of unusual toiletry conceits. Merchandise that is different—that combines beauty and individuality with saleability. This unlimited array awaits your inspection in a price range which will astound you.

No. 17 — retails $1.00		No. 24 — retails $1.00
No. 18 — " 1.00		No. 25 — " 2.00
No. 19 — " 1.00		No. 26 — " 5.00
No. 20 — " 2.50		No. 27 — " 3.00
No. 21 — " 1.00		No. 28 — " 5.00
No. 22 — " 2.50		No. 29 — " 5.00
No. 23 — " 1.00		

IRVING W. RICE & CO., 15 W. 34ᵗʰ St. N.Y.C.

1934

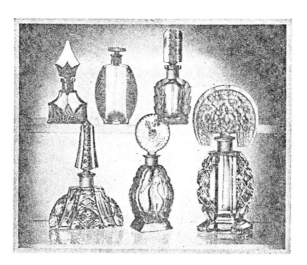

Values Extraordinary In Koscherak Perfume Bottles

*B*OHEMIAN Glass Perfume Bottles of finest quality, workmanship and style. Numbers illustrated to retail (top row) 50c to $1.25; (bottom row) $1.50 to $6.00. Most styles are crystal and in various lovely colors. Many other styles available in popular price ranges. Quotations will be made promptly on request.

• • •

KOSCHERAK BROS., INC.
IMPORTERS SINCE 1887
129-131 FIFTH AVENUE, NEW YORK
PERMANENT DISPLAYS
CHICAGO—W. C. Owen, Inc.   LOS ANGELES—R. F. Tallmadge
1520 Merchandise Mart   833 So. St. Andrews Place
EASTERN STATES: H. Herbert Ladd, Traveling
SOUTHERN STATES: R. B. Fore, Jr., Traveling

95

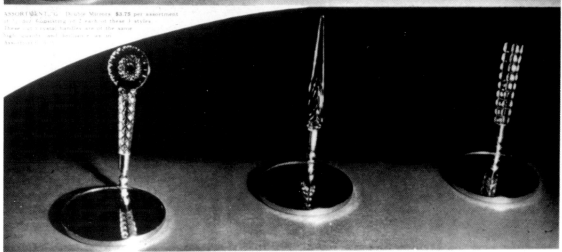

DE BOER & LIVINGSTON, INC.
IMPORTERS

14-16 EAST 30th STREET   PACIFIC COAST OFFICE
NEW YORK, N. Y.   633 SOUTH HILL STREET
                                LOS ANGELES, CALIF.

Please order in packing units to insure safe delivery. If merchandise received is not to your entire
satisfaction you may return same at our expense.
We would appreciate your sample orders.

97

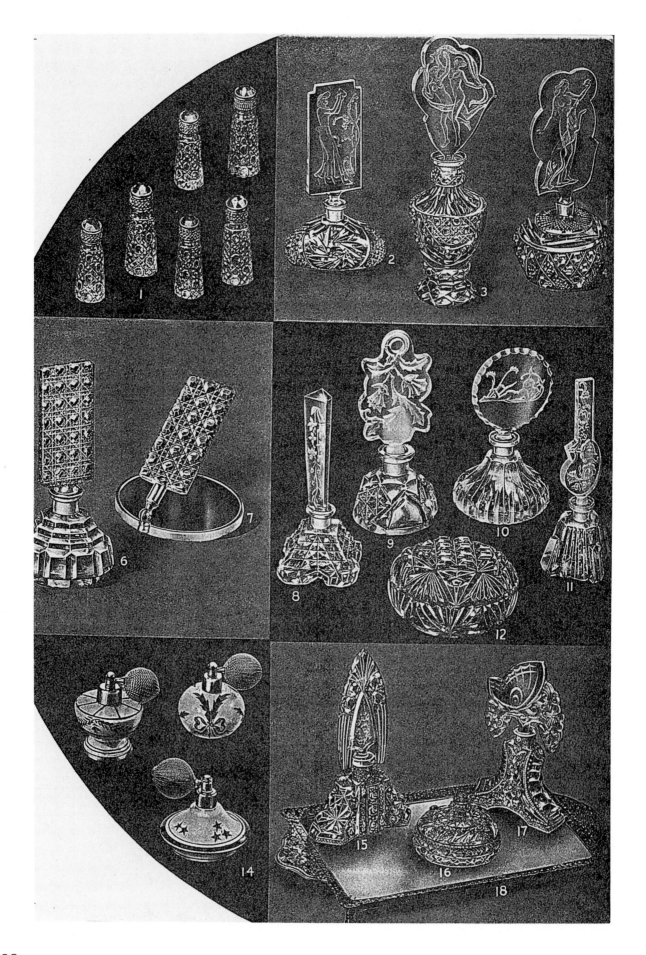

On to New Triumphs

with

IRVING RICE

Each season buyers look to Irving Rice for those irresistible toiletries that are profit-and-volume leaders.

The new imports of Bohemian hand-cut crystal shown here are chosen from a collection of dazzling beauty . . . fashion-right . . . fully worthy of the enviable IRICE reputation.

Suggested Retail Prices:

1	.25	8	1.00	15	10.00
2	3.00	9	1.00	16	6.00
3	6.00	10	1.00	17	10.00
4	5.00	11	1.00	18	4.00
5	.50	12	1.00	19	1.00
6	2.00	13	Set 1.00	20	1.00
7	2.00	14	.89		

IRVING W. RICE & CO.
15 W. 34th Street, New York City

1936

with smarter, better merc...

LET RICE IMPORTS BUILD YOUR STORE'S PRESTIGE

It's an IRICE Year

Every IRICE import sparkles with smartness and ingenuity of design. They are merchandised to fit your price lines...to move fast...to yield you a handsome profit.

Retail Prices

1, 2, 3, 4, 5, 6, 7, 8, 9, 10, 11, 12, 13, 14				$1.00
15	$2.00	20	$10.00	25 . . 2.00
16	3.00	21	7.50	26 set . 25.00
17	3.00	22	6.00	27 tray . 20.00
18	4.00	23	5.00	28 . . 35.00
19	5.00	24	6.50	

IRVING W. RICE & CO.

15 WEST 34TH STREET • NEW YORK CITY

Perfume Bottle, retail $3

Perfume Bottle, retail $1

Perfume Bottle, retail $2

Lead Crystal Set, retail $25

Perfume Tray, retail $25

Magnifying Mirror, retail $2

Powder Bowl, retail $1

Perfume Lamp, retail $10

Perfume Atomizer, retail $7.50

Perfume Bottle, retail $7.50

Perfume Bottle, retail $5

Perfume Bottle, retail $5

A 1936 De Boer & Livingston advertisement.

Typical selections from our extensive line of perfume bottles, powder bowls, atomizers, lead crystal sets, perfume lamps, perfume trays, dresser sets, magnifying mirrors, and novelties.

We cordially invite you to visit our showrooms on your next trip to New York.

DE BOER & LIVINGSTON, INC., IMPORTERS

Bottles

These exquisite styles in imported perfume bottles have been "hand-picked" from our vast stocks for your autumn and Christmas gift selling . . . They represent a comprehensive variety of the most attractive styles in the fastest selling price ranges . . . and are arranged for convenient selection direct from this page . . . The difficulty of keeping complete stocks on these imported gift items at this season makes advisable an immediate order.

McCOY, JONES & WESTLAKE, Inc.
Merchandise Mart • Chicago

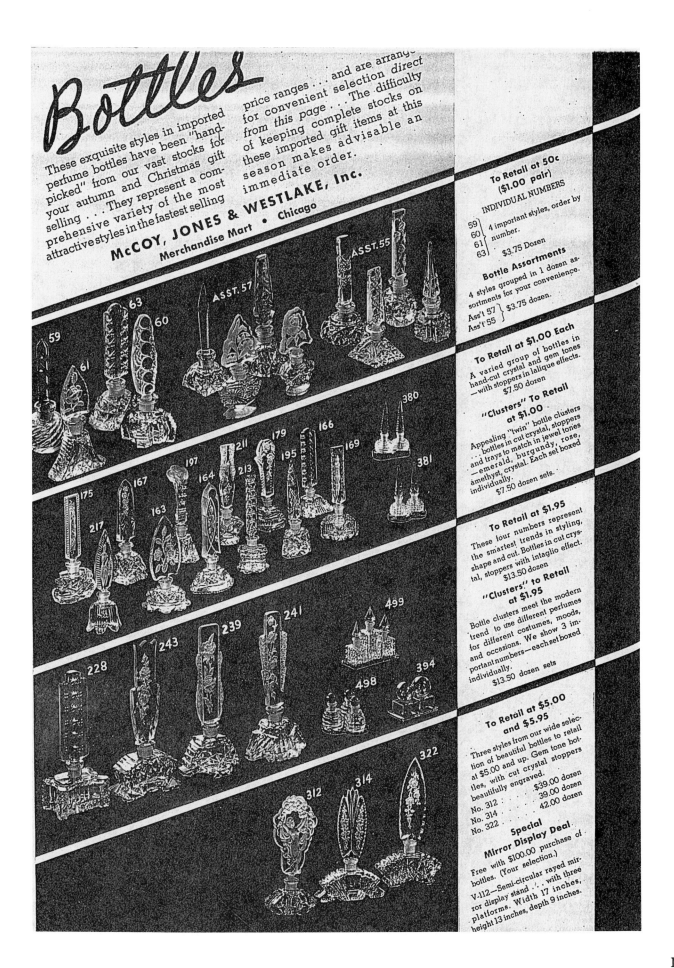

To Retail at 50c
($1.00 pair)
INDIVIDUAL NUMBERS

59 } 4 important styles, order by
60 } number.
61 }
63 } $3.75 Dozen

Bottle Assortments
4 styles grouped in 1 dozen assortments for your convenience.

Ass't 57 } $3.75 dozen.
Ass't 55 }

To Retail at $1.00 Each
A varied group of bottles in hand-cut crystal and gem tones —with stoppers in lalique effects.
$7.50 dozen

"Clusters" To Retail at $1.00
Appealing "twin" bottle clusters . . . bottles in cut crystal, stoppers and trays to match in jewel tones —emerald, burgundy, rose, amethyst, crystal. Each set boxed individually.
$7.50 dozen sets.

To Retail at $1.95
These four numbers represent the smartest trends in styling, shape and cut. Bottles in cut crystal, stoppers with intaglio effect.
$13.50 dozen

"Clusters" to Retail at $1.95
Bottle clusters meet the modern trend to use different perfumes for different costumes, moods, and occasions. We show 3 important numbers—each set boxed individually.
$13.50 dozen sets

To Retail at $5.00 and $5.95
Three styles from our wide selection of beautiful bottles to retail at $5.00 and up. Gem tone bottles, with cut crystal stoppers beautifully engraved.

No. 312 . . . . $39.00 dozen
No. 314 . . . . 39.00 dozen
No. 322 . . . . 42.00 dozen

Special Mirror Display Deal
Free with $100.00 purchase of bottles. (Your selection.)
V-112—Semi-circular rayed mirror display stand . . . with three platforms. Width 17 inches, height 13 inches, depth 9 inches.

103

Bottles!

by

MARSHALL FIELD AND COMPANY

Importers

● We've scooped the market again this year—with a line of exquisite imported bottles that fairly take your breath away. Some of these have already made names and gratifying sales for themselves—but we have ordered plenty (thousands and thousands of dozens!) to take care of orders and re-orders for immediate and Christmas selling. The bottles shown here are a few of the best numbers—but they would make a good, representative stock.

Upper left triangle The four bottles in the two top rows retail at $1, and the three below form an assortment of three styles and assorted colors to the dozen; retail, 50¢

Lower right triangle These retail from $2 to $5 Others in the same price range, not illustrated, are legion in style and coloring!

Central panel The famous Lilliputian bottles for Dram Sales of perfumes! The 11 numbers on the top four rows and the 13 numbers on the lower four rows make up this group, and retail at 50¢ without perfume. Centered in this panel are 'families' of bottles - little groups in three sizes—and an eye-catching Bridge Quartette on a colored glass plaque.

Prices on request !

ARISTO BOTTLES

MARSHALL FIELD & COMPANY
Manufacturers · Converters · Importers
222 North Bank Drive — CHICAGO
Madison Ave. at 35th St. — NEW YORK

A 1934 Marshall Field & Company advertisement.

*From a Paul A. Straub &
Co. advertisement.*

PERFUME BOTTLES

5 New Shapes with

up - to - date

Stoppers

Special at $7.80 doz.

Packed 1¼ doz. assorted

VANITY SETS OF DISTINCTION

These three piece vanity sets in an overlay glass are
available in three new soft colors;—powder blue,
salmon pink and a Bristol white. These sets may be
had in two decorations;—with wreath and stars
(astral) or star design only as illustrated.

Order now to assure prompt deliveries.

$2.50 per set, net.

CZECHO-SLOVAK GLASS PROD. CO.
45 EAST 34th STREET   NEW YORK CITY

Sales Representatives

Geo. F. Bassett & Co., 225 Fifth Ave., N. Y.
H. F. MacKenzie Co., 1592 Merchandise Mart, Chicago
Alfred Rasmussen, 233 Grant Ave., San Francisco, Cal.

Actual Size

1936

Rice Goes the Limit!

Satin Finish Czecho-Slovakian Crystal

COTTON PICKER

29c
Retail

An outstanding promotion for early
Fall business at a history-making
price! Lovely boudoir tones . . .
crystal, rose, blue, green, amber.

IRVING W. RICE & CO.
15 West 34th St.   New York City

105

THE IRICE HIT

"Follow the Leader"

IRICE once more brings you sparkling crystal Toiletries that sell!

Retail Prices:

1, 2, 3, 4, 5, 6, 7, 8, 9, 10, 11, 12, 14		$1.00
13 . . . . $2.00	20 . . . . $6.00	26 . . . . $8.00
15 . . . . 1.50	21 . . . . 4.00	27 . . . . 7.00
16 . . . . 3.00	22 TRAY . . 20.00	28 . . . . 7.50
17 . . . . 2.00	23 . . . . 9.00	29 . . . . 8.00
18 . . . . 1.50	24 . . . . 7.00	30 TRAY . . 12.00
19 . . . . 5.00	25 . . . . 12.00	31 SET . . 20.00

FOR NEWNESS, FOR SMARTNESS, FOR ORIGINALITY THE LINE IS **RICE**

A JOYOUS EASTER! FILL
YOUR COUNTERS WITH
LOVELY NEW SPARKLING
IRICE IMPORTS! YOUR
CUSTOMERS WILL BE
THRILLED WITH THE VALUES!

ALL ITEMS PICTURED ARE
DOLLAR RETAILERS!

ORDER BY NUMBER

IRVING W. RICE & CO.
15 W 34   N Y C

ARISTO CRYSTAL CUT GLASS BOTTLES

1018   1002

1013

1000

1005

7035   1008   1012   1027   7037

1019

1014   1026   1017   1033   1037   1032   1035   1034

GROUP A ABOVE

1021   1003   1004   1040   1042   1039   1006

1009   1020   1043   1041   1038   1015

GROUP B   Tray 7000

ALL BOTTLES IN THIS
PANEL
Can Be Retailed for
$1.00 Each
Available in Solid Crystal
and Colors
Rose, Blue, Champagne
Price $7.20 per Dozen

All Bottles in this Panel
and Make Up Mirrors
With Handles to Match
Bottle Stoppers
Can Be Retailed for $1.00
Crystal and Colors
Rose, Blue, Champagne
Price $7.20 per Dozen

All Bottles in this Panel
Can Be Retailed for 50c Each
Solid Crystal and Colors
Rose, Blue, Emerald, Amethyst
and Champagne
Sold by Individual Pattern or Ass'ts
Each Group A and B Packed
2 Dozen Assorted
Price $3.75 Doz.|$43.20 Gross

Upper Right Bottle
To Retail for $2.0
Upper Left Twin S
To Retail for $1.
Set of Bottle, Powder
Mirror Plaque
Sold in Sets or Indiv

ASSORTMENT H. Perfume Bottles. $7.50 per assortment of one dozen. Consisting of two each of these six styles. Crystal and assorted colors.

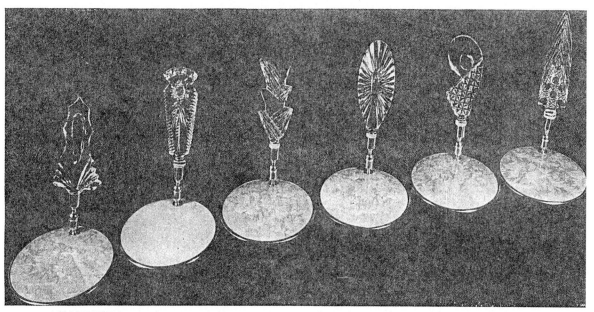

ASSORTMENT I. Magnifying Mirrors. $7.50 per assortment of one dozen. Consisting of two each of these six styles. Brilliant cut crystal handles with swivel attachment. Inserts in pastel shades.

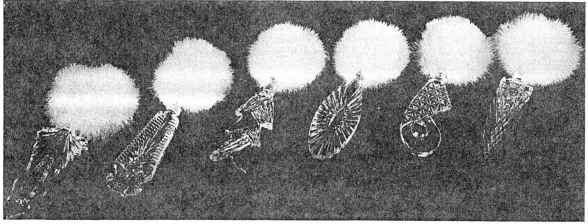

ASSORTMENT J. French Swansdown Puff Patters. $7.50 per assortment of one dozen. Consisting of two each of these six styles in full pastel color range. A unique innovation in first quality French Swansdown with cut crystal handles attached. Each piece attractively boxed and sealed with cellophane.

De Boer & Livingston advertisement.

A 1937 advertisement for The Premier Co.

Another 1937 advertisement for Premier.

Devoted

TO THE SUBJECT OF
VANITY AND VALUE

1938

25th Anniversary Special

3 PIECE VANITY SET

TO RETAIL AT $1 THE SET

The most exceptional value Irving Rice has presented in twenty-five years. This lovely imported set . . of the finest quality Bohemian crystal . . consists of two perfume bottles and matching powder jar. Stoppers in charming "vase and flower" motif are hand cut and hand polished. Crystal, rose, blue, green, amber. To enhance the beauty of this set a 7" x 14" mirror plateau may be had at small additional cost. . ¼ solid crystal. Packed 25 dz. sets to a case in assorted colors

IRVING W. RICE & CO.
15 WEST 34TH STREET   NEW YORK CITY

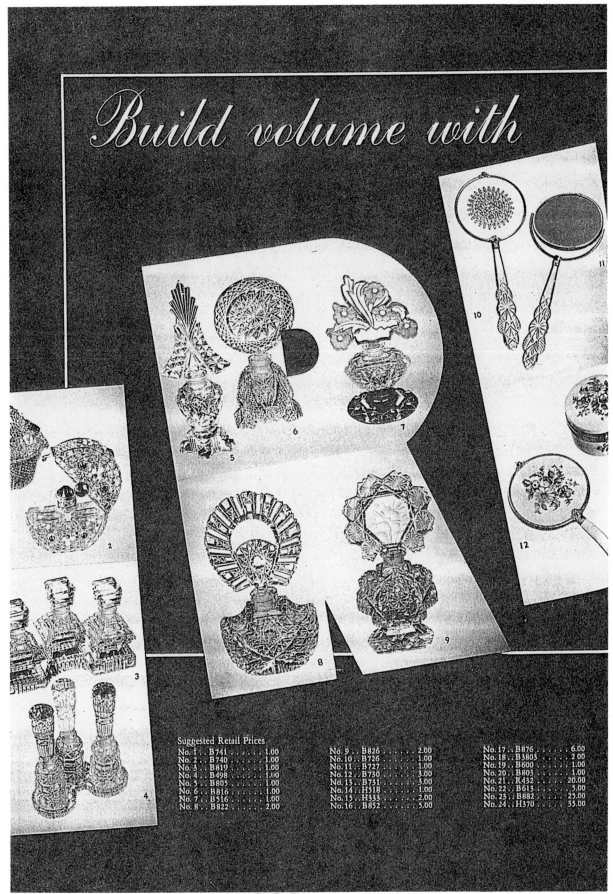

Build volume with

1938

Imports

First with the new, the unusual . . at a price that sells . . the *Irice* Fall collection of hand-cut Bohemian crystal surpasses even the triumphs of former years in originality, beauty of design *and value!*

IRVING W. RICE & CO.
15 WEST 34TH STREET · NEW YORK CITY

PREMIER *Presents*

1938

A clever adaptation of the most expensive perfume trays. Crystal clear polished glass with set-in mirror bottoms. Attractively designed—of generous proportions

Now — for the FIRST TIME produced to retail for as little as ....$1·59
An outstanding value—

To insure quick delivery rush your requirements. Individually boxed—Tray measures 8½ x 14½—Order our No. 4057.

No.				Retail
1	-	-	-	$1.00
2	-	-	-	1.00
3	-	-	-	5.00
4	-	-	-	1.00
5	-	-	-	1.00
6	-	-	-	1.00

A random selection from our current lines . . . Sparkling crystal and colors . . . Hand cut and polished . . . Czecho Slovakian imports . . . Complete price range.

We also manufacture the one outstanding, moderately priced line of 24 kt. gold-plated dresser sets and accessories.

The PREMIER CO., Inc., 29 W. 35th St., New York City

No.				Retail
7	-	-	-	2.00
8	-	-	-	2.00
9	-	-	-	2.00
10	-	-	-	3.50
11	-	-	-	5.00
12	-	-	-	5.00
13	-	-	-	10.00

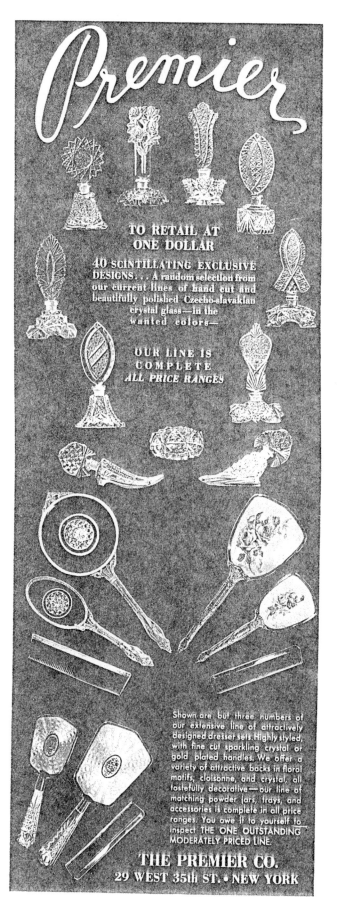

1938

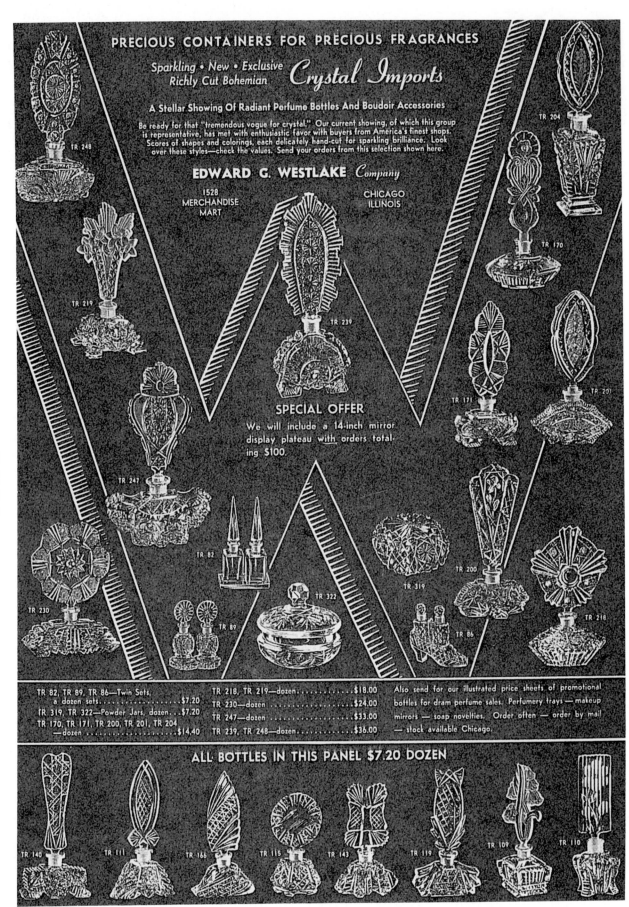

PRECIOUS CONTAINERS FOR PRECIOUS FRAGRANCES

Sparkling • New • Exclusive
Richly Cut Bohemian *Crystal Imports*

A Stellar Showing Of Radiant Perfume Bottles And Boudoir Accessories

Be ready for that "tremendous vogue for crystal." Our current showing, of which this group is representative, has met with enthusiastic favor with buyers from America's finest shops. Scores of shapes and colorings, each delicately hand-cut for sparkling brilliance. Look over these styles—check the values. Send your orders from this selection shown here.

EDWARD G. WESTLAKE *Company*

1528
MERCHANDISE
MART

CHICAGO
ILLINOIS

SPECIAL OFFER

We will include a 14-inch mirror display plateau with orders totaling $100.

TR 82, TR 89, TR 86—Twin Sets, a dozen sets...........$7.20	TR 218, TR 219—dozen.............$18.00	Also send for our illustrated price sheets of promotional bottles for dram perfume sales. Perfumery trays—makeup mirrors — soap novelties. Order often — order by mail — stock available Chicago.
TR 319, TR 322—Powder Jars, dozen...$7.20	TR 230—dozen $24.00	
TR 170, TR 171, TR 200, TR 201, TR 204 —dozen $14.40	TR 247—dozen $33.00	
	TR 239, TR 248—dozen..........$36.00	

ALL BOTTLES IN THIS PANEL $7.20 DOZEN

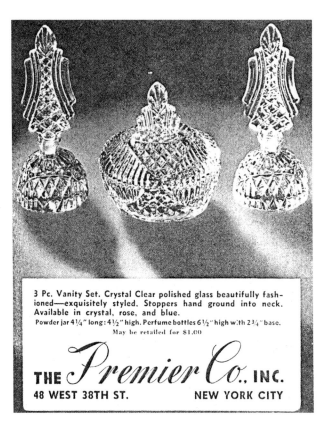

3 Pc. Vanity Set. Crystal Clear polished glass beautifully fashioned—exquisitely styled. Stoppers hand ground into neck. Available in crystal, rose, and blue.
Powder jar 4¼" long; 4½" high. Perfume bottles 6½" high with 2¾" base.
May be retailed for $1.00

THE *Premier Co.,* **INC.**
48 WEST 38TH ST.   NEW YORK CITY

1939

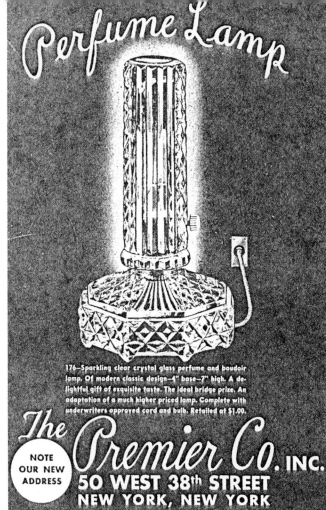

176—Sparkling clear crystal glass perfume and boudoir lamp. Of modern classic design—4" base—7" high. A delightful gift of exquisite taste. The ideal bridge prize. An adaptation of a much higher priced lamp. Complete with underwriters approved cord and bulb. Retailed at $1.00.

The *Premier Co.* **INC.**
NOTE OUR NEW ADDRESS
50 WEST 38th STREET
NEW YORK, NEW YORK

Opalescent Hobnail glass vanity set.

Also Showing At

The Gift & Art Center, 225-5th Ave., New York, Room 400. The line is represented by: Geo. F. Bassett & Co.

An international selection of better gifts, artwares, and replicas of antique glass and china.

Attention:
Buyers visiting the New York World's Fair, our headquarters exhibit is on your way to the Fair grounds, just 4 blocks from the Pennsylvania Station.

CZECHO - SLOVAK GLASS PRODUCTS CO.

45 EAST 34th STREET   NEW YORK CITY

IRICE PRESENTS

"The Duchess"

VANITY SET

BOTTLE HEIGHT
9½ inches high
POWDER JAR OPENING
4 inches across
OVAL TRAY
9 inches by 20 inches

1940

VALUE HEADLINER FOR *Easter* **PROMOTION**

Meet *"The Duchess"*... blue-white crystal bottle and jar set... hit success in the several selected metropolitan stores in which it was introduced.

Made in an American Factory by artisans who for years operated the largest perfume bottle manufactory in Czecho-Slovakia.

Offer your customers this value headliner for Easter. They'll GO for *"The Duchess."*

BOTTLE, JAR...
Retail .... $1⁰⁰ each
MIRROR TRAY...
Retail .... $6⁰⁰ each

IRVING W. RICE & CO., INC., 15 W. 34 ST., N.Y.C.

830 (Left). Opaque black, very unusual bottle with open space through it decorated with two lounging nudes, mismatched stopper, bottle only 6".

831 (Lower Left). Black opaque, strange Hoffman designed bottle & stopper each with two frosted glass clinging monkeys on a bare tree branch in metal, 7-1/2".

832 (Lower Right). Black opaque, metal work set with imitation opals, 5".

834 (Right). Amberina, rare, Ingrid design, flower basket stopper, three cupids on base. No marks, 6-1/4".

835 (Lower Left). Pink, nude dauber/grey, jeweled filigree, this Hoffman bottle came in many sizes, colors, and finishes, 8".

836 (Lower Right). Clear and frosted, butterfly on large tulip stopper, 8-1/2".

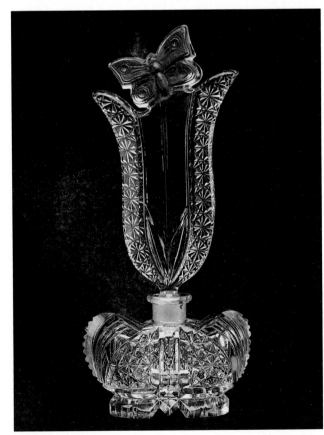

837. Opal green, trinket or jewel box, man playing a stringed instrument looks at a ship in the distance, 7" x 5-1/2".

838 (Lower Left). Close-up of a Hoffman nude dauber. The nudes came in many different styles and sizes, 5-1/2".

839 (Upper Right). Clear and frosted, card or pin tray, Hoffman design, nude blowing bubbles at bird, 5" across. **(Lower Right).** Clear and frosted, pin, ash, or salt tray, three Grecian women, 3-3/4".

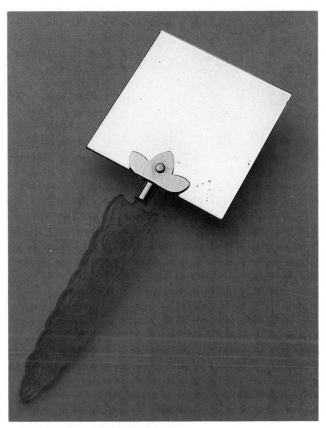

840 (Upper Left). Grey, flowers on stopper, short haired deco nude holding a flower on bottle, Ingrid design, 5-3/4".

841 (Upper Right). Hand mirror, blue glass handle, molded rose design, 11".

842. Amber, jeweled filigree, glass coaster, angel with woman holding a bow and arrow, 3-1/2". Amber, perfume funnel, molded roses, 2-1/2". Amber, hat pin, dancing lady with knotted scarf, 6".

124

BOTTLE TIPS

- The best cleaning agents to use inside a perfume bottle to remove hardened perfume and other stains are fingernail polish remover, lime-away toilet bowl cleaner, or denatured alcohol.

- A toy baby bottle brush is perfect for scrubbing the inside of a bottle clean.

- Use a plastic sink liner when cleaning your bottles to prevent chipping or breakage.

- Hand-stained or painted decoration should be checked for color fastness before you clean a bottle with water or a cleaning agent.

- Sometimes the misty bloom on the inside of a bottle can be removed with liquid bleach. Pour the bleach into the bottle and let stand overnight.

- Keep in mind that Irice and Morlee marketed bottles made in both Europe and America. A paper Irice or Morlee label on an item does not necessarily mean it was made in Czechoslovakia.

- Occasionally only part of an acid mark is visible on powder boxes and bottles with cut bottoms.

- Opaque black glass made in Czechoslovakia was actually a deep amethyst, blue, or green colored glass.

- Some collectors with small children or clumsy visitors use dental wax to hold the bottle stoppers in place to prevent damage.

- Color can make the same bottle look quite different. The thinner the glass, the lighter a color will usually appear.

- Bottles which still have the original dauber usually cost 10% to 20% more than bottles without one.

- To prevent breaking a dauber, the stopper should be lifted straight out of the bottle.

- A collector should not pass up a fine bottle because of small chips. A glass repairer can usually smooth them away very easily.

- For a correct stopper fit, the frosted stopper dowel should sit below the bottle lip and be even with the frosted part of the neck.

- Get to know dealers who specialize in bottles or Czechoslovakian glass. In the long run they will provide the best help and advice in adding to your personal collection.

BIBLIOGRAPHY

Czechoslovakian Glass 1350-1980. New York: Dover Publications, Inc. 1981.

Forsythe, Ruth. *Made in Czechoslovakia.* Marietta, Ohio: Richardson Printing Corp., 1982.

Heacock, William. "Czechoslovakian Glass," *Collecting Glass,* Volume 2. Marietta, Ohio: Richardson Printing Corp., 1985.

North, Jacquelyne. *Perfume, Cologne & Scent Bottles.* West Chester, Pennsylvania: Schiffer Publishing, 1986.

North, Jacquelyne. *Commercial Perfume Bottles.* West Chester, Pennsylvania: Schiffer Publishing, 1987.

Sellner, Christine. *GLAS in der VERVIELFALTIGUNG.* Bergbau-Undindustriemuseum Ostbayern, 1986.

For further reading on perfume bottles I highly recommend the *Perfume & Scent Bottle News* published quarterly. Send a check for $15.00 to: Perfume & Scent Bottle Collectors, P.O. Box 85824, Las Vegas, Nevada 89185.

GLOSSARY

APPLIED - Decorative glass that is added after a bottle is removed from its mold.

CASED - A blown glass with two or more layers of different colors, including clear glass. While the glass was still hot, the layers were fused one inside the other.

CLEAR - Transparent glass.

CRYSTAL - A brilliant transparent glass which contains a high amount of lead oxide.

CUT CRYSTAL - Crystal decorated with faceted designs cut by a rotating wheel.

DAUBER - Device for applying perfume.

DOUBLE STOPPER - Stopper decorated with intaglio designs on both sides of the glass.

DOWEL - The cylindrical base of a stopper that fits into the neck of a bottle (also called the tongue).

DRAM - One-eighth of an ounce.

DRESSER SET - Matching brush, hand mirror, and comb.

EMBOSSED - Patterns or marks that project slightly from the surface of the glass.

ENAMEL - Decorative substance colored with pigments derived from metallic oxides fused to the surface of glass or metal by firing.

FIGURAL - Bottle or stopper decorated with a human figure.

FILIGREE - Lace-like ornamental work of delicate or intricate design made of metal.

FROSTED - Glass with a frost-like surface made by exposure to hydrofluoric acid.

FUSE - Add or blend together by heating or firing.

HAND FINISH - Smoothing and polishing the glass by hand on a felt or wooden polishing wheel.

HAND PAINTED - Application by hand of lacquer or oil-based colored pigments without subsequent firing.

HOBNAIL - Overall decorative glass pattern of small raised knobs known technically as "prunts."

INTAGLIO - Decorative design pressed into the glass below the surface to leave a reverse relief.

JEWEL - Imitation precious or semi-precious stone made of glass.

LIP - The projecting curved edge or rim at the top of the bottle neck.

MOLD - Metal form into which molten glass is poured.

MOLD-BLOWN - Process of blowing molten glass into a patterned mold that shapes and decorates it in one step.

MOLD MARK - See "seam."

NECK - The narrow upper part of a bottle.

OPAQUE GLASS - Highly colored glass with little or no translucency.

OPENWORK STOPPER - A molded stopper with openings through the glass.

PIERCED - See openwork stopper.

PRESSED GLASS - Glass formed in a mold by mechanical pressure rather than by blowing.

RELIEF - Projection of a sculptured design from the surface of the glass.

SEAM - Ridge left on the surface of a bottle formed in a mold.

SHOULDER - Sloping sides of a bottle below the neck.

SICK GLASS - Glass that has been damaged by external factors.

TOILET SET - Three or more matched pieces sold as a set for use in a bathroom.

TRANSPARENT GLASS - Glass that is easy to see through.

TWO-PIECE BOTTLE - Bottle that came in two parts connected by some type of adhesive.

VANITY SET - Usually two perfume bottles and a powder box in a matching pattern sold together. Trays, atomizers, and other items were sometimes included in a set.

~ ADDENDUM ~

843. Nude dauber perfume bottles in various sizes.

Contributions by

KEN LEACH
RUTH A. FORYSTHE
MADELEINE FRANCE

844. Hoffman Oriental designs in black crystal (from left): malachite Chinese fret jewel, white enamel, 5-1/4 "; pierced lady and floral stopper, jade glass ornaments, 8-3/4"; jeweled, Persian fret ornament, 4-3/4"; "snuff bottle" shape, 3-3/4".

845. Hoffman bottles, black crystal: (left and right) glass jewels, 5-3/4", 4-1/4".; (center) enameled trim, 7".

WHEN LUXURY WAS A NECESSITY
CZECHOSLOVAKIAN BOTTLES IN AMERICA

KEN LEACH   PHOTO CREDIT: MORRIS LANE

The never-ending fascination with decorative Czechoslovakian vanity crystal continues to gain momentum, as the uninitiated eagerly discovers its beauty. Not surprisingly, the greatest majority of these objects are to be found in the United States, some having been designed as early as the late teen's to captivate and satisfy the unrestrained tastes of the post-war American woman. Like other women around the world, she had experienced her first liberating encounter with financial and social independence while the men had been away fighting for their countries. Newly emancipated, with her hair stylishly short and dress less inhibiting, she looked for novelty and modernity in her surroundings to throw off the modes of the past.

847. Deeply cut bottle, pierced stopper, modernist style classic figure, 6-5/8".

846. Intaglio partial nude stopper with overflowing basket of flowers, 7-3/4".

Throughout the 1920s and 1930s, if she was among those lucky enough to be relatively unaffected by the war, the crash, and the Depression, these fashionable crystal objects helped offer a psychological cushion against whichever harsh realities affected her world.

For centuries Bohemian glassware had enjoyed international appeal, with exports to India, South America, and equatorial Africa around 1700, and distribution in the United States by 1740. After World War I, as Czechoslovakia was established and its glass industry began to flourish, the political climate and financial instability of the world greatly narrowed its potential export market. As nations suffered subsequent decades of communism, fascism, and world economic recession, an estimated 70% of

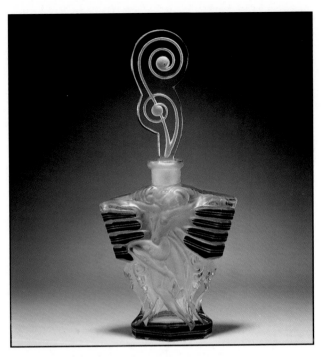

848. Butterfly lady, black enamel, antennae stopper, 8-1/2".

849. Unidentified commercial bottle, molded two-figure stopper, 5-1/2".

Czechoslovakia's glass production from 1920 to 1938 was exported to America, the major consumer, as well as to England, Australia, and South America. The artificial boom experienced in the United States between 1927 and 1929 realized unparalleled spending on personal luxuries.

Throughout our short history, and entering the 20th century, Americans have alternately imitated the French and English tastes, adding the exoticism of the Orient by the 1920s. With no royalty to revere, we noblized the accomplishments of celebrity and wealth. We took our fashion cues from across the footlights, and looked to our captains of industry to model our lives after. As they decorated their homes in the current styles of European society, one particular furnishing found its way into most every middle to upper class household in America from 1910 to 1950 - the dressing table. Used by the privileged in Europe, the Middle East, and throughout Asia, it had appeared in various forms for more than 3,000 years.

Seated at her mirror, however modern

the 20th-century female, she could not escape the imagined reflection of an ancestress going through a similar daily ritual of grooming. These dressing or "vanity" tables laden with brilliant crystal bottles, jeweled and filigreed brush sets, trays, frames, boxes and various accessories, gave women a sense of glamour, of civilized elegance, and perhaps more importantly, of domain. They afforded an escape from her designated kitchen and parlor responsibilities. These bathroom and boudoir retreats were her undisputed territory, her oasis of self indulgence and pampering, where she could quietly linger and gaze over a tablescape of pleasing shapes, colors and finishes. In reaching for various powders and fragrances, she enjoyed the use of each product more because of its beautiful crystal container.

While the popular use of Czechoslovakian vanity decoration was greatly influenced by the fantasy life styles portrayed in magazines and in motion pictures, it was propelled by the recent art form of department store window display, and the vehicle

850. "Carved" malachite glass elephant with riders, elephant stopper, 5-1/8".

851. Hoffman bottle, glass jewels, bakelite stopper, 5".

852. Czech group with ladies in, as, and on stoppers (from left): yellow bottle, pierced lady stopper, 8-5/8"; amber lady stopper, clear base, 6-1/4"; clear Hoffman bottle, aqua nude dauber, 7-1/4"; Ingrid tray, leaping gazelle handles, length 19".

853. Deep red-orange crystal bottle. exaggerated ivy stopper, jeweled ornament consisting of clear red stones, carved bakelite roses, 7".

of catalog shopping. From the early 1900s, ladies magazines showed the latest trends in decoration by focusing on the homes of the rich and famous. By the late teen's, large undecorated or enameled Czech toilette sets consisting of many pieces were featured, with the more elaborate intaglio stoppered bottles not appearing until the late 1920s through the 1940s. Film related magazines often posed favorite starlets in front of bottle laden vanities, and by the 1940's bottle ads would even appear in mens magazines before particular holidays.

In the 1920s, "personal shopping" offered by magazines such as *Vogue* and *Harpers*, provided New York department store access to the most remote areas of the country, as did the direct catalog sales method, which also offered payment by installment, and featured Czech bottles into the 1950s. Those store windows displaying perfume bottles with a wax mannequin frequently drew such tremendous crowds that the police were called upon to

854. Czech group (from left): clear base, pink "Lily-of-the-Valley" stopper (identical to colorless model by R. Lalique, 1931), 4-1/4"; green "tiara" stoppered bottle, 8-1/2"; pierced clear "tiara" stopper, pink base, 6"; blue bottle, kneeling lady and floral stopper, 8-1/4"; green "kissing butterflies" stopper, jeweled base, 8-1/4"; yellow bottle, birds building nest stopper, 7-1/2"; amber Hoffman bottle, "Venus de Milo" stopper, 7-1/4".

break up the sidewalk blockade. In 1925, the respected display artist Jules Brodeur (Canadian born, and student of Barbier), stated that his most successful American department store windows involved the use of Bohemian crystal toiletry items on a French boudoir dressing table.

Spanning the years from silent to talking pictures, costume and set designers combined historic reference with the latest art trends and products, to create stylish surroundings for characters that would be emulated throughout the world. American women looked to fashion their modest bedrooms into versions of the sumptuous boudoirs occupied by vamps and queens seen on film. Today these surviving screen images serve to document the progression of styles developed by various glass makers. Seen as background in films prior to 1922 are French and Bohemian crystal objects, some opaque and others with metal overlay. Throughout the mid-1920s the accessories tend to be of Venetian and French manufacture until 1927, when

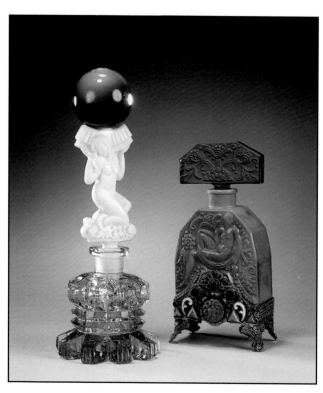

856. Hoffman bottles: (left) Opaque pale green nude with ball stopper, pink base, 7-1/4"; Amethyst stopper, malachite base, jeweled and enameled holder, 5-1/2".

Czech glass reappears in the form of architectural elements, lighting fixtures, perfume bottles and vanity pieces.

Although the majority of decorative Czech perfume bottles were manufactured to be sold empty, two applications of commercial usage arose in the 1920s. Just prior to the 1925 Decorative Arts Exhibition in Paris, a number of commercial perfumers had begun to commission specific designs to be produced for the general marketing of their fragrances. Earliest examples reflected the fluid art nouveau style of soft lines, acid etching, and delicate surface staining. Soon after, lines hardened into geometrics, and color was introduced into the glass or as surface enameling. Unlike the larger stoppered bottles of the 1930s and 1940s, which were afforded by the average pocketbook at one or two dollars, the commercially used bottle filled with fragrance retailed from $25 to $200, with advertised emphasis on the crystal. A list of

855. Amethyst crystal, enameled and jeweled ornaments: (left) portrait on ivory, 7"; (right) 5-1/2" .

some perfume companies supplied would include: Passy, Paul Jones, Langlois, Youvenel, Molinelle, Vionnet, Rosine, Schiaparelli (presentation domes only), Selog, Vyrobce, Dralle, Le Clairac, Fournier, Prince de Chany, Lalanne, Jeurelle, Cassel, D'Astra, Conde, Cleopatra, De Folet, Sajor, Notre Dame, De Kama, Max Factor, and Ahmed Soliman.

By 1928, specially ordered quantities of recognized models were purchased by exclusive retailers for limited deluxe packaging of their own fragrances. The elaborate showrooms of make-up artist Max Factor in Hollywood, and of perfumer Ahmed Soliman in Cairo, both offered a wide range of Austrian mounted Czech toilette garniture made of gold dore bronze heavily encrusted with glass jewels and pearls, as well as perfumes in bottles designed by Heinrich Hoffman (see page 18). The Apollo Studios of New York, a bronze firm working in similar style to the Tiffany Studios in the 1920s, also used Hoffman bottles in their own heavily bronze mounted dresser sets, featuring enameled details or faux jewels.

Heinrich Hoffman (1875-1939) was prominent among glass makers at the luxury level of vanity glass production. He and later son-in-law Henry Schlevogt (1904-1984) manufactured from their own designs, and those of famed contemporary artists. Hoffman's reputation in glass, known as the specialist for articles made of jet black crystal, was established in Paris just prior to the glass work of Lalique. A box he made in 1913 is in the permanent collection of The Musée de Arts Décoritifs, and prior to 1917, his production in Gablonz of iridescent glass similar to that of Louis Comfort Tiffany, won him the

857. Malachite glass group, c.1930 (from left): Pyramid bottle with nudes, female mask stopper, 6-1/2"; Bird bottle, jeweled collar, bakelite stopper, 7"; Elephant on "carved" orb, 5-1/4".

858. Lapis glass group, c. 1930 (from left): cherry motif bottle, bird stopper, 4-1/4"; modern disk pattern, 6"; deer and foliage, floral stopper, 6-1/4".

award of "Imperial Counselor" by Austrian Emperor Franz Joseph.

Hoffman's vanity pieces followed the art deco ethic in shape and subject, but echoed an art nouveau stylization late into the 1920s. Production was handled by contract factories and cottage finishers in Gablonz, with jeweled bronze mounting accomplished in Austria, and sales transacted in Paris. The realistic glass jewels manufactured in Gablonz are legendary and were used also in the thinner brass Czechoslovakian mountings of the 1930s, as well as eventual use in costume jewelry by names such as Chanel, Dior, Schiaparelli, and Hattie Carnegie.

Two of Hoffman's major accomplishments, the process for intaglio molded stoppers, and his "nude dauber" bottles with suspended interior figures, were in production prior to 1927, when future son-in-law Henry Schlevogt came to Hoffman to learn the mechanics of mold pressing glass. Schlevogt had been looking to reintroduce

an opaque colored glass developed in the 18th century, that gave the appearance of carved stone, but up to this time no one had shown an interest outside of industrial marble manufacturers looking to imitate agate. Now together, they worked to formulate various stone colors and molds for vanity items. Combination opaque bases with transparent stoppers in various hues, two-color all molded bottles and stoppers, and bottles and stoppers of different glass type were all products of this time.

Three years after his wife's death and his departure from Hoffman, in 1933 Schlevogt perfected his stone glass with the help of Walter Riedel from Polaun. Now remarried, and using molds designed by Hoffman and by exceptional modern artists of renown, he found great success with the "Ingrid" line through domestic and international expositions from 1934 to 1939. Schlevogt took part in the 1937 Worlds Fair in Paris and won the Grand Prix for three of

"Ingrid" advertising postcard, c. 1936. Example of architectural use of stone glass wall covering.

859. Detail of "Ingrid" crystal wall tiles.

The Women, MGM, 1939. Phyllis Povah, Rosalind Russell and Joan Crawford with Houbigant, LeLong, Lentheric, Weil, and Corday bottles, as well as the fictitious Summer Rain. Credit: Photofest.

A still from My Past, 1931. Joan Blondell (seated left) sits with a nude dauber bottle at each shoulder. Bebe Daniels is on the right. Credit: Photofest.

his sculptural pieces. Earlier at the 1925 Exposition, the exterior of the Czech Pavilion had been covered entirely in red glass panels, and now Schlevogt demonstrated the proposed architectural application of jade (malachite) stone glass tiles as interior wall covering, but there is no documentation of its subsequent utilization.

When the Germans occupied Czechoslovakia the following year, Schlevogt's production was greatly reduced and exports to the United States ceased. When the Russians over took Czechoslovakia in 1944, Schlevogt's possessions were confiscated, his wife humiliated, and he was sentenced to be sent to Siberia. Powerful friends in America and France intervened and instead, he was incarcerated in Czechoslovakia until 1948. Upon his release, the same friends arranged visas for he and his wife to go to Austria, and from

1950, until his death at 80, he ran a wholesale business on the Rue de Paradis in Paris handling the finest quality crystal of major designers.

Thousands of technicians, hundreds of craftsmen, and numerous artists were responsible for the production of Czech vanity objects, yet only a handful have been identified. With the invasion by Germany in 1938, those Czech designers and mold makers that did not escape the occupation were reduced to laboring in factories selected to remain in production, as Germans were placed in supervisoral positions and the identity of those responsible for previous artistic endeavors was obliterated. In 1996, at what had been the most productive of the early manufacturing facilities (including works by Hoffman and Schlevogt), original pencil sketches were found in an abandoned office still pinned to

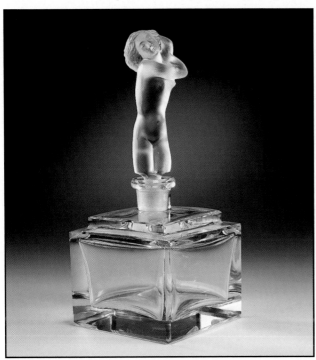

860. Ingrid bottle used in 1939 movie, "The Women" (MGM), 6-1/2".

the wall above a work table of broken maquettes (plaster models for the mold makers). Each drawing of a bottle, box, or vase bore the original Czech designer's signature with lines scratched through, and over it a substituted German name.

Throughout following decades under communist rule many bottle designs continued to be produced, but almost exclusively in clear frosted crystal. In the 1950s various large pieces from the original Ingrid catalog were molded in light pastel shades and in the dichromatic glass, "Alexandrite." This transparent crystal, patented in 1902 by Thomas Webb & Sons of England, was first produced in Czechoslovakia by Moser in 1924. A prize winner at the 1925 Paris Exhibition, it had the ability of changing color depending on its light source, whether direct or shaded, and from artificial to natural. These items tended to be thick walled and came in vibrant colors including a red to orange, a lavender to turquoise, and a yellow to green. The Ingrid "stone" line, which continued only in limited green pro-

duction in a fire polish finish unlike the originals, became popular in domestic sales, and was exported in small quantities internationally until the early 1980's.

Max Factor was the first to import Hoffman pieces into Hollywood, attracting the attention of actresses and set designers. Soon, Czech items would be seen decorating movie sets in all of the major studio's productions. Two early film appearances of numerous Hoffman vanity objects occur in the Warner Bros. releases of "My Past" (1931) and "Jewel Robbery" (1932).

In 1939, when a scene in "The Women" (MGM) required a certain bottle to be its focus, an undistributed Ingrid design was disguised with a label, tinting, and plastic umbrella to appear as a commercial bottle containing the nonexistent fragrance "Summer Rain." From 1919 to the 1950s there is seldom a dressing table seen on film without a decorative accessory made of Czechoslovakian crystal.

Fashion designer Coco Chanel said that "Luxury is a necessity that begins where necessity ends." This could not have been truer or more necessary to the emotional well being of thousands of Americans during difficult times. The beauty and artistry of these objects will never betray the unfortunate circumstances under which many were created, and they will continue always to enrich the lives of those who choose to collect them.

If collecting them is a luxury, then all the better to believe they are a necessity!

REPRODUCTIONS

RUTH A. FORSYTHE, PHOTO CREDIT: JAROSLAV KARBULKA

Most collectors of Czechoslovakian perfume bottles and boudoir accessories search for objects made from 1918 through 1938. Those 20 years were a boom time for Czechoslovakian exports to many countries, with the lion's share going to the United States. The glass was beautiful, of excellent quality, and endless variety. All this and still affordable!

From 1938 through World War II, importers could no longer obtain Czechoslovakian perfume bottles. Although luxury goods were not in great demand during the war years, dealers commissioned glass manufacturers in this country to make bottles. Many were copies of Czechoslovakian designs.

When Czechoslovakia was under communist control from 1948 to 1989, exports

861. Two nudes on molded bottle (new 1998).

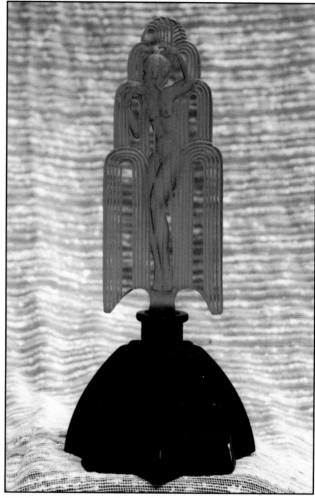

862. Nude in a fountain on a molded bottle (new 1998).

to the United States were quite limited and, at times, non-existent. Bottles made in the Czech style by other countries lacked the quality and detail of the earlier Czech wares. There was no concern about these reproductions because few collectors were interested in perfume bottles of this type. Copies were made as late as 1995, but they were pressed glass of inferior quality that would mislead only the most uninformed collector.

Opaque bottles, vases and accessories have been made since 1950 and are still being made. The green is often called malachite because the color resembles the min-

863. Kneeling nude with chrysanthemums on cut bottle (new 1998). Stoppers are to be notched like the 1918-1938 stoppers.

eral of that name. However, it is easy to tell the difference between the old and new malachite pieces, especially when they are examined side by side. Since 1993, imports have been marked Czech Republic or Slovak Republic.

During World War II, the Germans were reported to have stripped a majority of the Czechoslovakian factories of metal to use for the production of ammunition. Many old molds were undoubtedly destroyed during this period. For obvious reasons, in those few glass factories that were kept in operation for German profit, only some of the metal was confiscated. Since the Czech Republic became an independent nation, numerous molds for perfume bottles have been found. At present, about 80 different bottles are in the process of being reissued. Several have already appeared in the marketplace and others will be manufactured by early 1999. The most costly will be cut and polished bottles, with the same shapes being available in frosted glass.

A company in Wisconsin that produces and imports new bottles is Boheme. These wares will be marked "Boheme" either with an acid mark or a paper label, and will be sold as new reissues.

The bottles produced between 1918 and 1938 are found with an acid mark, "Made in Czechoslovakia" or "Made in Czecho-Slovakia." The mark may be in an oval, a circle or just a straight line. However, some of the old pieces are not marked because they may have been part of a vanity set. When sold in sets, only one piece had to be marked.

Another mark is "Ingrid," seen on early pieces as an acid signature, and later on a paper label. Still another mark for the Hoffmann designed pieces is a tiny embossed or cut butterfly. There is an excellent explanation of Ingrid and Hoffman starting on page 18 of this book. Note that some of the new bottles are being marked "Made in Czechoslovakia" in an acid stamp similar to the originals, but much larger in scale. Others are being acid stamped "Lalique". These marks are added by dishonest sellers, not the manufacturers.

Reproductions are made to sell in volume and to make a good profit. They are not intended to deceive. It is not important

864. Kneeling nude with chrysanthemums on frosted bottle (new 1998).

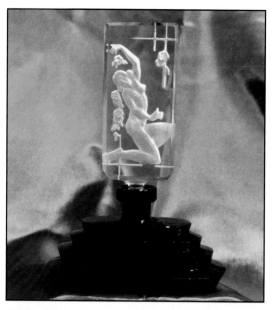

865. Kneeling nude on molded bottle (new 1998).

866. Lady sitting on a baluster admires a peacock, cut bottle (new 1998)

867. Harem dancer on cut bottle (new 1998).

868. Scantily draped nude with fish (Siren) on cut bottle (new 1998).

that they be an exact copy because they are made to appeal and sell to the general public rather than to a few collectors. For the reasons of a less-skilled labor force and a higher cost for materials and manufacture, items made at a later time are never exactly the same as the originals.

An excellent example of this is illus-trated by comparing items #819 and #820. #819 was made in Czechoslovakia, while #820 is acid stamped Japan. They were not trying to fool anyone—just copying a good design to make money. The stopper on the Made in Japan bottle looks the same at a glance, but is actually quite different. The girl's face is almost blank; her hair is differ-

869. Jitterbug couple on frosted bottle

870. Two nudes with pearls on cut bottle (new 1998).

ent, as are body detail and the surrounding foliage. The shape of the stopper is even different. However, in viewing them separately, a novice could be fooled.

Everything ages. Time and the elements affect wood, paper, metals, fabrics and, yes, glass. Decorated glass is especially apt to lose its bright new finish. Objects often have small chips or flakes, and the bottoms become scratched and dull from being moved from one place to another. Many of the perfume bottles of the 1918-1938 time period had drop stoppers, but often the small rods have broken off. On those with jeweled filigree, the brass is no longer shiny and bright.

We want to collect old things, but like for them to look new. A good glass repair man can make a bottle look almost new. There isn't anything wrong with removing small chips, but the bottom of a piece should never be polished. After all, the bottom doesn't show, and it is the best place to look for signs of age. One certainly would never remove the acid stamp that reads "Made in Czechoslovakia."

Purse bottles with jeweled filigree are currently being advertised by a large company whose business is reproductions. To be certain you are getting Czechoslovakian purse bottles, look for a tiny oval nameplate on the side of the neck of the bottle (see item #636). If the bottle doesn't have the nameplate or show evidence that it has been broken off, be careful.

Reproductions are not a problem if you know your subject. Most dealers are honest and reliable and won't hesitate to tell you the truth about what they are selling. Their reputation is important to them and they will gladly give a written guarantee.

An important question concerning reissues or reproductions: Will these new items change the monetary value of a collection of old perfume bottles? It has been proven many times that reproductions do not necessarily undermine the value of the original items. In some cases, these items actually increase in popularity and value. A few examples of this trend are Tiffany lamps, Burmese glass, pattern glass, and Depression glass. The list is endless.

The old saying remains true: "Imitation is the most sincere form of flattery."

144

CZECHOSLOVAKIAN
PERFUME BOTTLES IN PERSPECTIVE

MADELEINE FRANCE   **PHOTO CREDITS: PAT OLSEN, RANDALL MONSEN, MADELEINE FRANCE**

871. An array of nude daubers.

INTRODUCTION

Two major factors have added to the scarcity of Czechoslovakian perfume bottles in the antiques marketplace today:

First, collecting interest was inspired by the photographs and information offered with the first edition of this book, *Czechoslovakian Perfume Bottles and Boudoir Accessories*, in 1990; and the two volumes by Ruth Forsythe, *Made in Czechoslovakia*, in 1982, and *Made in Czechoslovakia, Book 2*, in 1993. Each of these references presented an eye-opening variety of colorful bottle designs.

The second factor was the founding of the International Perfume Bottle Association in 1989, which brought together collectors of similar interests from around the world. In 1990 the first "all perfume bottle show" took place in conjunction with the

872. Rare opaque black and red art deco nude perfume, 5".

IPBA annual convention in San Francisco. It was at this and subsequent exhibitions that many new collectors, who were intrigued and charmed by these beautiful bottles, came into the market.

When the borders of the Czech Republic opened in 1989, collectors went to Prague and the surrounding areas to find these perfume bottles. Unfortunately, if they had read articles on this collectible, they would have been aware that almost all of the "fancy" figural and jeweled perfumes were made for export to the United States. Since the U.S. was the greatest importer of Czech glass items, these bottles are also scarce in Germany, France, Belgium, and other European countries.

With 2,000 glass-related companies operating in the Bohemian area, the amount of all types of crystal goods exported to the United States was staggering. Some interesting facts have come our way since this book was originally published. Here are some exportation statistics covering the Bohemian industry from 1920 to 1930:

41,000 tons of beads
11,000 tons of buttons
200,000 tons of stones
110,000 tons of jewelry

These figures actually represent less than 40% of the Bohemian industrial output. Decorative objects for the home accounted for a large share of the remaining 60% made for export.

Hoffman-Schlevogt

At the turn of the century, Paris was considered the artistic capital of the world. Heinrich Hoffman, who lived there most of his life, was influenced by the art that surrounded him. It was his goal to place artistically valuable glass on the market. With his eye for art, the stereotyped floral designs did not meet his high standards. Hoffman was striving to create fantasy in glass, and today's collectors still view his creations as modern and daring in their

873. Cobalt blue molded Hoffman bottle with art deco nudes, 6".

146

874. Rare purple figural with women's profiles in molded, frosted glass, 6-1/2".

875. Clear bottle with two frolicking nymphs, 8".

design. While he worked in Paris, his wife, Josephine, ran the business in the City of Gablonz. Thus, Hoffman carried the spirit of Paris to Czechoslovakia.

Henry Schlevogt, the son-in-law of Heinrich, worked in the family business. Among his many contributions, Schlevogt developed unique types of marbleized glass—lapis lazuli (blue), malachite or jade (green), jet or onyx (black), ivorine (white), azurite (turquoise) and cinnebar (red).

After his wife died in childbirth in the 1930s, Schlevogt left the Hoffman firm and rejoined his father's business for himself. There he made buttons, Venetian-type glass beads, glass eyes, buckles, necklaces and other jewelry.

Even after leaving the Hoffmans, Schlevogt worked very closely with his late wife's family. He was given some perfume bottle molds by his former father-in-law, Heinrich. When he started

producing bottles in opaque glass with the mark "Ingrid," named after his daughter, Hoffman's signature butterfly mark can sometimes be visible on these pieces. In 1934, the year the "Ingrid" Collection was first produced, Schlevogt exhibited his marbleized glass perfume bottles in a show in Leipzig, Germany and won a prize. He was 30 years old at the time.

Neither Hoffman nor Schlevogt operated a glass manufacturing plant. Rather, they designed molds, contracted with a machine shop to have them built, and then had the glass produced by a firm such as Riedel in Polaun. However, the shops of Hoffman and Schlevogt were equipped to do the finishing work. They also employed cottage workers for certain tasks. There were many different artisans who played a part in the finishing work, such as polishers, engravers and enamelers.

876. Rare jewel mounted tantalus containing three clear and etched perfumes, 4".

877. Black opaque with clear stopper and rare silver-colored mountings, 6-1/2".

878. Black opaque with jeweled mounts, clear and frosted stopper, 8-1/2".

879. Green jeweled perfume with peacock stopper, 4".

880. Light blue glass with enameled and jeweled mount, 5".

881. Malachite jeweled deluxe, 9".

882. French empire-style stopper with Hoffman butterfly in amber glass with jeweled decor, 5".

883. Light blue, frosted pair of nudes holding a bottle with filigree and porcelain medallion, 6" (see also #590).

884. Rare amethyst colored nudes with jeweled medallion, 5-3/4" (see #883 and #590).

885. Jeweled azurite deluxe, 9".

886. Enameled and jeweled with braided tiny seed pearls, 6".

887. Amethyst bottle with jeweled and enameled decoration, 6".

Hierarchy of
Czechoslovakian Perfume Bottles

To aid the collector in determining the value of Czechoslovakian perfume bottles, the following chart is offered. This ranking begins with the most desirable and continues to the more common and less-valuable bottles.

A. Nude three-dimensional dauber
   1. Colored stopper and bottle
   2. Colored stopper, clear bottle
   3. All clear, stopper and bottle

B. Figural opaque
   1. Rare combinations of two or three opaque colors in one item
   2. Red and black opaque blended in one design
   3. Rare opaques
      a. Light pink (coral)
      b. Light brown (agate)
      c. Dark brown (agate)
      d. Orange (coral)
   4. White (ivorine)
   5. Red (garnet)
   6. Opalescent (opal)
   7. Azurite (turquoise or aqua—light or dark)
   8. Black (jet)—top and bottom
      a. Black with ivory opaque stopper
      b. Black with red stopper
      c. Black with malachite stopper
      d. Black with clear or frosted stopper
   9. Lapis Lazuli opaque
   10. Jade—no marbling
   11. Malachite

C. Three-dimensional figural stoppers
   1. All colored—stopper and base
   2. Opaque base (usually black), clear stopper
   3. All clear

D. Figural intaglio molded stoppered perfumes
   1. Colored glass stopper with matching base

888. Very rare Czech atomizer with colored enameling of art deco style nude, 4".

   2. Colored bottom only, stopper clear with enameled staining
   3. Colored bottom, clear stopper
   4. All clear, stopper and base

E. Faceted or geometric-cut stopper and base, same color
   1. Colored bottom, clear stopper
   2. All clear

Here are some important points to remember:

It is extremely rare to see one color in the stopper and another in the base. Black opaque bases prove the exception, however, as they can be found with different colored stoppers.

Some opaque black perfumes were enhanced with ivory elements, such as a stopper with an ivory insert surrounded by marcasites in a brass holder with an enameled art-deco design. This provided a nice complement to the popular French art deco furniture of that period.

A black and red opaque combination

889. Black opaque glass three-piece Austrian set with dark brown bakelite feet, bronze mounts with black enamel and green cabochons.

890. Boudoir set in black enamel with amber bottles and amber glass jewels, signed Austria.

was produced by using red opaque glass as the base color in the mold. The mold was then allowed to cool so that it could be opened and the glass removed. The black background areas were painted with a combination of a metal oxide powder, a flux (which is a form of powdered glass), and a liquid binder. The piece was then reheated

891. Very rare black opaque perfume, clear and frosted stopper with Austria's bronze enameled ormolu, 8".

892. Austrian two-piece set with enameled filigree and cabochon jewels.

893. Black opaque with pink-faceted jewels and white enamel, mounting signed Austria, 5" (*see fig. 832*).

894. Rare, large-size, malachite glass on wood jewel box with foiled green mirror. Shows Myth of Perseus and Pegasus, 14" x 7".

895. Signed Austria black amethyst glass with French empire-style filigree and Bacchus-head stopper in jade opaque.

896. Crystal and non-crystal nude daubers

at a specific temperature to achieve the end result—two-colored opaque glass. These colors can reach different shades depending on how often the oxide mixture was applied, and how many times it was fired.

This method of coloring glass was used hundreds of years ago, particularly in stained glass windows. To achieve this two-colored opaque glass there were many extra time-consuming steps to be followed. It is no wonder that they are scarce.

An important note concerns bottles in the ranking that have been embellished in special ways. If applied jeweled filigree or enameled brass mountings adorn a perfume, it elevates that bottle to the top of its category. Several rare examples of jeweled perfume bottles are illustrated in this book.

Jeweled or Filigree-covered Bottles

The metal filigree work that we see on perfume bottles was the same type of metal used in jewelry. All Czech metal work was done by hand until the mid-1920s. The metal workers were called "gürtlers." There were 928 registered gürtlers employed in the Gablonz area of Czechoslovakia with about 4,000 others working for them.

The main and preferred metal was a copper and zinc alloy called "tombac." This material was used because it was pliable and relatively inexpensive. Gürtlers would also use brass and bronze. Because of the various guilds established before 1900, however, gurtlers could not work with precious metals such as silver or gold.

Tombac was cut into strips and placed in an iron mold or stamping tool that had been engraved very precisely into a working pattern. Some of these patterns were designed by Joseph Hillebrand (1865-1931), who established an "estamperie" in 1898. These elements had to be very exact and looked like decorated wire. The steps of

897. Large Austrian bronze frame with semi-precious stones and enamel.

898. Austrian bronze frame jewelled with enamel

899. Various jeweled Austrian/Czech boudoir items.

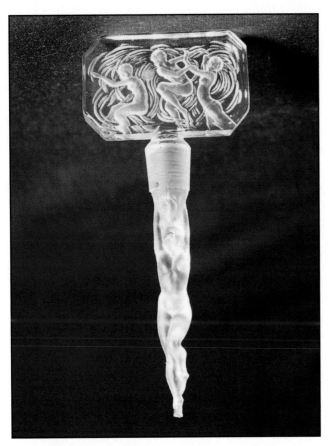

900. Rare stopper used for an English commercial perfume, 3-1/2".

901. Jeweled nude dauber, 8".

this process were as follows:

1. Basic pattern stamped out.
2. 10 to 12 solderings done, depending on number of elements.
3. Enameling or gilding applied.
4. Setting of stones.
5. Placing the metal mount on the bottle.

Each piece had to go through skillful hands that were responsible for their own specialty. Although this method of decoration had been employed for many years, the first known advertisement in the United States for jeweled or filigreed bottles was in 1934.

Nude Dauber Perfume Bottles

The three dimensional "nude dauber" perfume bottle is among the rarest to be found. In all likelihood, the majority of these were produced by the Heinrich Hoffman factory. If you look very carefully at the top of the nude dauber, you will sometimes find a molded butterfly mark. There was a great deal of craftsmanship involved in the making of this stopper. Because of its fragile nature, especially at the tip of the feet, you can imagine how many of them were broken while being removed from the mold. A very expensive loss of time and effort.

These precarious and exquisite perfume bottles were produced in a wide spectrum of colors: vaseline, peach pink, deep rose, light and dark blue, lime and dark green, amber, violet, opaque black, grey, and clear. Those adorned with ormolu, or enameled and jeweled metal fittings, are the most sought after. Most of these fittings were manufactured in Austria and later in Czechoslovakia. The heavier metal mountings were marked "Austria" in block letters.

The design of these mountings was

probably a collaboration between Hoffman and Schlevogt. Schlevogt's background involved knowledge of the manufacture of jewelry. Glass jewels were incorporated into the filigree mounts. These cabochons and faceted stones complemented the color of the bottle and magnified its beauty. Often the stones were carved into flowers or other designs of art deco origin.

These perfume bottles range from 4" to 9" in height. The nude figure may have several different poses, such as with arms raised over her head or crossed over the body. The top of the stopper can also have several different designs. The most common is a flat polished top. Other variations are a ball of molded flowers, a fan or fishtail, or even a swan. Stoppers with a molded-flowers top have an indented horizontal line about one-third up from the base of the ball. In many cases this is where the stopper was cut to produce the flat-top design. In other cases the indented groove was used to hold a metal decoration to complement the metal fitting on the base of the bottle.

From an advertisement in a cosmetic trade magazine in the 1930s, a non-crystal nude dauber perfume bottle was offered by Ramses, Inc. with *eau de toilette* for $1.00. Because the quality of these mass-produced bottles is poor, they are easily identified. The molding is not very crisp or refined; the colors are weak and washed-out looking. Most important of all, there was a cork going around the tongue that went into the neck of the bottle to seal the contents. There is an indentation to allow for this cork. This was much less expensive than trying to fit a stopper to each bottle when they were exported.

A better quality crystal version of the nude dauber bottle was introduced by Max Factor in 1928. The DeKama Perfume Company also used the crystal version in 1932, with their product selling for the costly sum of $125.00 a bottle! Into the 1940's various firms used many different

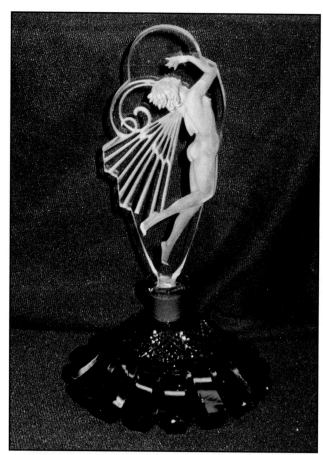

902. Rare root beer colored base, stopper enhanced with colored staining, 8-1/2"

opaque and colored Czechoslovakian perfume bottles to promote the sale of their colognes and perfumes.

Figural Stoppered Perfume Bottles

Flowers, butterflies, birds, mythological figures, cupids, male and female figures abound in these reverse molded stoppers. Whether they are romantic couples in court dress, ladies in turn-of-the-century costume, or single and double nude figures, these figural stoppered perfumes are highly sought after by collectors today. Around 1925, Heinrich Hoffman utilized the method of reverse molding these designs onto both sides of the stoppers. The design was pressed into the glass and then acid etched.

There were many procedures to follow in the finishing of these stoppers and, because of their difficulty, less than one half survived to completion:

157

1. After taking the piece from the mold, excess glass from the overflow must be removed, which resulted in the loss of approximately 30% of the blanks.

2. Fitting of stopper to the bottle, with the loss of 20% of the remaining blanks.

3. Cutting of contours or design. Up to ten different polishing wheels must be used.

4. Rough cutting and polishing of the back of the stopper.

5. Initial overall polishing.

6. Entire stopper is dipped in acid and becomes frosted

7. Final polishing. Both front and back flat areas are polished to clear. This process leaves the intaglio design frosted. This is done no less than three times.

There are rare times when colored enamel staining has been applied to the reverse molded figure in the stopper. This was done for the overall harmony and visual balance of an individual piece. A few examples of this type of detail finishing to enhance the beauty of a perfume bottle are silver staining on a clear stopper with a black base, yellow to amber staining on a clear stopper with a dark brown base, and peach to light red staining to complement a peach base. Deluxe figural stoppers in the same color as the bottle are extremely rare.

From the beginning of the 20th century, styles were changing from art nouveau to art deco. In order to keep up with modern tastes, both Hoffman and Schlevogt hired the most talented of contemporary artists to design the engravings or carvings for the stopper molds.

Famed sculptor and artist, Josef Drahonovsky of the Prague School of Art, is responsible for many designs, notably fig. 403 (p. 54). This style is representative of his work. Frantisek Pazourek, one of Drahonovsky's former students, worked for Hoffman from 1929 to 1931. Even after leaving the firm to follow other artistic pursuits, he continued to produce designs for them until 1939. Pazourek undoubtedly created many figural stoppers.

Artists Adolf Beckert and Alexander Pfohl also designed for the firm. Pfohl, whose renderings of birds and flowers were famous, returned to his hometown of Novy Bor in 1928 and taught at the Glass School. All of the above artisans did not just work on perfume bottles. but also vases, boxes, and other glass items.

Reproductions

As early as 1850 in France, reproductions of Louis XIV, XV and XVI furniture were in existence. When there is a popular demand for an item, be it an antiquity or not, look-alikes seem to appear in the market.

We saw a resurgence of malachite glass items at the end of the 1960s and beginning of the 1970s. The consensus is that these were reproduced in the late 1950s, as we see from the catalog reprints on pages 83-88. However, since the Czech Republic has been established, many new glass factories have been opened. The malachite and lapis glass items that have appeared in the last few years must be examined very carefully. Also, a new opaque color has recently been seen—light to dark brown—in floral and figural designs.

These are some characteristics of the newer bottles:

1. Color—deep color with only a slight marbleized effect.
2. All—over dull appearance to glass—or the opposite, very slick and shiny.
3. Visible and pronounced mold marks.
4. Mold areas not crisp, details are worn out.
5. Molded figures not polished to high light design.
6. No wear marks or scratches on the bottom.
7. Insides of the items, such as a vase or box, have no marbleized appearance; it almost looks spray painted.

When the figural stoppered perfume bottles began appearing at wholesalers and gift shops, they were easy for a collector to spot because of their inexpensive-looking molded bases. Upon close examination of the stopper, the following became apparent:

1. Lack of sparkle or luster to the glass.
2. Edges beveled very inconsistently.
3. Residue in reverse molding.
4. Figure not acid etched but sand blasted.
5. Missing very fine details in the design.
6. Small dowel or "tongue," finished very crudely.
7. No applied dauber.

Note: daubers are now being easily applied by glass repairmen. Don't buy a bottle thinking that it is old just because it has a dauber.

903. Reproduction with new cut glass base.

904. Reproduction in color of #579 (these are also reproduced in malachite and brown opaque.

905. Reproduction in color with new cut glass base.

159

The most noticeable characteristic is the bottle itself. Of course, a new stopper can be married to an old bottle, but most cannot since there are not enough old bottles available.

Over the last year or two, some of the above deficiencies have been rectified. Because of an apprenticeship program established in the factories, many young artisans are now learning the fine art of polishing, etching, and finishing glass. The new figural perfume bottles have a cut glass colored base with matching colored stopper and applied dauber. They are acid etched and look remarkably well finished. Because these deluxe stoppers are in color, not clear like the originals, we can easily determine that they are in current production.

Important new information: Figural perfume bottles that were traditionally done in clear and frosted are now appearing in malachite glass—for example #400 and #579.

Here are some guidelines when purchasing any antique item:

1. Purchase from a reputable source; look for quality, not a bargain.
2. Get a guarantee on your sales receipt from the seller as to the age of the item.
3. Make sure your receipt has the seller's name, address, and phone number.
4. If the price of an item is "too good to be true," examine it carefully.
5. Some estate sales are "salted" with new items that are not part of the estate. Buyer beware.
6. If there is something about the item that bothers you, pass it up.

Conclusion

Czechoslovakian perfume bottles, because of their beauty and bold sensual designs, have appealed to generations of women and men since they first appeared in our department stores and gift shops in the 1920s. It is no wonder that both collectors and dealers are so enchanted with them. They appeal to us not just because they are precious to behold, invoking the romanticism that perfume itself possesses, but they provide for us a visual history of style and taste from a bygone era.

Books have been published on all types of perfume bottles and auctions devoted only to the sale of perfumes are currently being held all over the world. This growing public awareness, coupled with the fact that perfume bottles are small and easily displayed, helps explain why so many connoisseurs of *objet d'art* have entered into this collecting field.

References

Jargstorf, Sibylle, *Baubles, Buttons and Beads*, Atglen, PA: Schiffer Publishing, 1993.

Leach, Ken, *Perfume Presentation, 100 Years of Artistry*, Toronto: KRES Publishing, Inc., 1997.

Sellner, Christianne, et. al. *Das Bomische Glas 1700-1950, Band VI*, Catalog by Passauer Glasmuseum, Germany.

Truitt, Robert and Deborah, *Collectible Bohemian Glass: 1880-1940*, self published, 1995.

Czechoslovakian Perfume Bottles and Boudoir Accessories

Revised Edition 1999 Price Guide

The values below are current estimates for the items shown in this book. Obviously, prices vary greatly throughout the United States and, indeed, elsewhere in the world. At best, these values are only approximations of what these bottles might bring at an auction, estate sale, or in a dealer's boutique. These prices are for perfume bottles in excellent condition, since damage or other flaws would lower an item's value appreciably.

Great care has been taken in assigning these prices, however the publisher and authors do not accept responsibility or liability for losses incurred by persons usually this guide, whether due to typographical errors or other factors.

Abbreviations: **a** - stopper altered   **m** - mismatch
                      pm - possible mismatch   **cp** - stopper in current production

FRONT COVER	19. - 275	53. - 85	87. - 125	121. - 275
A - 1850	20. - 125	54. - 175	88. - 200	122. - 250
B - 1250	21. - 125	55. - 50	89. - 285	123. - 150
	22. - 250	56. - 250	90. - 200	124. - 250
BACK COVER	23. - 250	57. - 325	91. - 250	125. - 175
A - 1650	24. - 150	58. - 250	92. - 295	126. - 375
B - 1450	25. - 550	59. - 125	93. - 225	127. - 125
C - 850	26. - 150	60. - 125	94. - 250	128. - 400
D - 1050	27. - 650	61. - 125	95. - 325	129. - 325
E - 950	28. - 375	62. - 275	96. - 325	130. - 375
F - 1250	29. - 1425	63. - 250	97. - 225	131. - 450
G - 1250	30. - 150	64. - 175	98. - 250	132. - 600
H - 850	31. - 275	65. - 150	99. - 250	133. - 650
I - 1200	32. - 150	66. - 150	100. - 275	134. - 325
	33. - 125	67. - 150	101. - 385	135. - 425
ITEM #	34. - 125	68. - 125	102. - 450	136. - 200
1. - 850	35. - 250	69. - 150	103. - 850	137. - 200
2. - 95	36. - 125	70. - 125	104. - 450	138. - 200
3. - 350	37. - 250	71. - 225	105. - 450	139. - 250
4. - 250	38. - 175	72. - 225	106. - 450	140. - 485
5. - 250	39. - 125	73. - 175	107. - 325	141. - 325
6. - 225	40. - 350	74. - 125	108. - 375	142. - 150
7. - 175	41. - 85	75. - 200	109. - 275	143. - 200
8. - 175	42. - 150	76. - 225	110. - 325	144. - 175
9. - 250	43. - 425	77. - 225	111. - 250	145. - 250
10. - 200	44. - 175	78. - 85	112. - 175	146. - 250
11. - 170	45. - 150	79. - 150	113. - 650	147. - 200
12. - 250	46. - 150	80. - 95	114. - 175	148. - 450 m
13. - 175	47. - 175	81. - 125	115. - 400	149. - 600
14. - 125	48. - 325	82. - 125	116. - 450	150. - 650
15. - 150	49. - 500 pm	83. - 500	117. - 300	151. - 125 pm
16. - 175	50. - 200	84. - 600	118. - 300	152. - 225
17. - 150	51. - 150	85. - 75	119. - 250	153. - 125
18. - 150	52. - 250	86. - 75	120. - 200	154. - 350

155. - 250	207. - 575	259. - 75	311. - 750	363. - 650
156. - 275	208. - 575	260. - 125	312. - 550	364. - 1900
157. - 185	209. - 450	261. - 75	313. - 750	365. - 2500
158. - 275	210. - 300	262. - 550	314. - 450	366. - 1000 cp
159. - 150	211. - 400	263. - 75	315. - 500 m	367. - 350
160. - 250	212. - 325	264. - 75	316. - 475	368. - 450
161. - 250	213. - 175	265. - 75	317. - 425	369. - 450 cp
162. - 250	214. - 250	266. - 175	318. - 350	370. - 650 cp
163. - 325	215. - 350	267. - 150	319. - 275	371. - 550
164. - 450 cp	216. - 250	268. - 125	320. - 275	372. - 450
165. - 450	217. - 300	269. - 175	321. - 275	373. - 285
166. - 425	218. - 650	270. - 275	322. - 125	374. - 425
167. - 250	219. - 650	271. - 225	323. - 250	375. - 225
168. - 450	220. - 450 cp	272. - 250	324. - 350	376. - 300
169. - 400 a	221. - 550	273. - 175	325. - 150	377. - 750
170. - 575	222. - 800	274. - 350	326. - 350	378. - 425
171. - 750 a	223. - 175	275. - 450	327. - 325	379. - 1500
172. - 450	224. - 250	276. - 325	328. - 250	380. - 425
173. - 375 pm	225. - 350	277. - 100	329. - 225	381. - 375
174. - 325	226. - 250 ea.	278. - 125	330. - 250	382. - 600
175. - 525	227. - 125	279. - 125	331. - 300	383. - 1200
176. - 450	228. - 450	280. - 150	332. - 425	384. - 2200
177. - 1400	229. - 450	281. - 200	333. - 300 m	385. - 250
178. - 250	230. - 250	282. - 125	334. - 325	386. - 1200
179. - 325	231. - 350 m	283. - 225	335. - 275	387. - 1000
180. - 275	232. - 175	284. - 150	336. - 400 pm	388. - 450
181. - 375	233. - 200	285. - 350	337. - 450	389. - 450
182. - 325	234. - 250	286. - 300	338. - 325	390. - 550
183. - 450	235. - 250	287. - 525	339. - 350	391. - 350
184. - 250	236. - 250	288. - 375	340. - 250	392. - 475
185. - 325	237. - 225	289. - 325	341. - 175 m	393. - 450
186. - 175	238. - 250	290. - 400	342. - 350 pm	394. - 850 cp
187. - 300	239. - 300	291. - 275	343. - 200 pm	395. - 475
188. - 350	240. - 300	292. - 325	344. - 225	396. - 375
189. - 300	241. - 75 ea.	293. - 275	345. - 250	397. - 450 cp
190. - 275	242. - 50	294. - 350	346. - 200	398. - 950
191. - 425	243. - 350	295. - 275	347. - 300	399. - 850
192. - 275	244. - 250	296. - 250	348. - 350	400. - 750 cp
193. - 300	245. - 250	297. - 125	349. - 325 m	401. - 1900 cp
194. - 250	246. - 50	298. - 250	350. - 150	402. - 450
195. - 225	247. - 450 m	299. - 125	351. - 200	403. - 750
196. - 250	248. - 75	300. - 450	352. - 250	404. - 850
197. - 200	249. - 125	301. - 800	353. - 500	405. - 850 cp
198. - 250	250. - 225	302. - 475	354. - 450	406. - 675
199. - 300	251. - 100	303. - 650	355. - 475	407. - 350
200. - 600 m	252. - 350	304. - 550	356. - 200	408. - 2000
201. - 1500	253. - 325	305. - 525	357. - 175	409. - 1050
202. - 1100	254. - 450	306. - 600	358. - 325	410. - 225 ea.
203. - 1500	255. - 450	307. - 750 m	359. - 200	411. - 175
204. - 850	256. - 50	308. - 450	360. - 225	412. - 450
205. - 800 m	257. - 125	309. - 650	361. - 425	413. - 650
206. - 575	258. - 175	310. - 850	362. - 2000 cp	414. - 225

415. - 75 ea.	467. - 225	519. - 325	571. - 250	623. - 75
416. - 75	468. - 285	520. - 225	572. - 250	624. - 125
417. - 350	469. - 225	521. - 325	573. - 350	625. - 125
418. - 300 m	470. - 375	522. - 300	574. - 475	626. - 125
419. - 175	471. - 350	523. - 225	575. - 625	627. - 125
420. - 450	472. - 300	524. - 325	576. - 575	628. - 125
421. - 600	473. - 300	525. - 350	577. - 3000	629. - 150
422. - 100 ea.	474. - 325 m	526. - 350	578. - 750	630. - 200
423. - 75	475. - 275	527. - 450	579. - 2000	631. - 150
424. - 90	476. - 175	528. - 375	580. - 2600	632. - 150
425. - 90	477. - 350 as is	529. - 275	581. - 550	633. - 225
426. - 85	478. - 200	530. - 450	582. - 650	634. - 225
427. - 85	479. - 650	531. - 300 pm	583. - 950	635. - 225
428. - 175	480. - 650	532. - 450	584. - 750	636. - 250
429. - 175	481. - 300	533. - 950	585. - 1700	637. - 125
430. - 125	482. - 400	534. - 275 pm	586. - 1600 pm	638. - 125
431. - 150 ea.	483. - 250	535. - 385	587. - 1200	639. - 150
432. - 225	484. - 300	536. - 450	588. - 2000	640. - 200
433. - 175	485. - 325	537. - 325	589. - 2000	641. - 225
434. - 375	486. - 300	538. - 375	590. - 2500	642. - 100
435. - 400	487. - 175	539. - 475	591. - 850	643. - 100
436. - 325	488. - 225	540. - 325	592. - 2250	644. - 175
437. - 125	489. - 175	541. - 350	593. - 1400	645. - 125
438. - 100	490. - 200	542. - 250	594. - 2000	646. - N/A
439. - 150	491. - 275	543. - 325	595. - 500	647. - 175
440. - 275	492. - 150	544. - 350	596. - 2000	648. - 125
441. - 300	493. - 275	545. - 325	597. - 75	649. - 75
442. - 275	494. - 300	546. - 300	598. - 75	650. - 75
443. - 300	495. - 275	547. - 175	599. - 75	651. - 75
444. - 300	496. - 350	548. - 275	600. - 75	652. - 75
445. - 300	497. - 375	549. - 175	601. - 175	653. - 100
446. - 175	498. - 350	550. - 300	602. - 75	654. - 75
447. - 275 m	499. - 300	551. - 400	603. - 75	655. - 75
448. - 200	500. - 350	552. - 150	604. - 75	656. - 125
449. - 225	501. - 275	553. - 200	605. - 200	657. - 450
450. - 250	502. - 200	554. - 350	606. - 75	658. - 75
451. - 200	503. - 395	555. - 200	607. - 100	659. - 75
452. - 275	504. - 250	556. - 425	608. - 100	660. - 125
453. - 300	505. - 225	557. - 525	609. - 75	661. - 125
454. - 200 pm	506. - 400	558. - 375	610. - 75	662. - 125
455. - 475	507. - 250	559. - 1050	611. - 125	663. - 150
456. - 550	508. - 350	560. - 650	612. - 125	664. - 75
457. - 490	509. - 325	561. - 1000	613. - 75	665. - 125
458. - 85	510. - 350	562. - 400	614. - 125	666. - 125
459. - 400	511. - 325	563. - 650	615. - 125	667. - 175
460. - 150	512. - 425	564. - 325	616. - 125	668. - 125
461. - 125	513. - 185 m	565. - 475	617. - 150	669. - 150
462. - 175	514. - 375	566. - 750	618. - 150	670. - 100
463. - 150	515. - 450	567. - 275	619. - 150	671. - 125
464. - 185	516. - 375	568. - 400	620. - 150	672. - 125
465. - 225	517. - 175	569. - 750	621. - 150	673. - 100
466. - 125	518. - 225 m	570. - 525	622. - 75	674. - 100

675. - 125
676. - 125
677. - 125
678. - 200
679. - 125
680. - 150
681. - 50
682. - 75
683. - 50
684. - 50
685. - 75
686. - 75
687. - 75
688. - 100
689. - 125
690. - 150
691. - 150
692. - 125
693. - 225
694. - 225
695. - 225
696. - 300
697. - 300
698. - 250
699. - 250 set
700. - w/#699
701. - 350 set
702. - w/#701
703. - 300 set
704. - w/#703
705. - 75
706. - 100
707. - 75
708. - 75
709. - 300
710. - 125
711. - 175
712. - 125
713. - 175
714. - 175
715. - 200
716. - 150
717. - 150
718. - 175
719. - 225
720. - 300
721. - 425
722. - 375
723. - 175
724. - 250
725. - 45
726. - 45

727. - 45
728. - 45
729. - 85
730. - 85
731. - 450
732. - 75
733. - 75
734. - 125
735. - 200
736. - 45
737. - 125
738. - 225
739. - 175
740. - 200
741. - 300
742. - 300
743. - 250
744. - 50
745. - 350
746. - 75
747. - 35
748. - 75
749. - 150
750. - 75
751. - 125
752. - 275
753. - 225
754. - 350
755. - 200
756. - 350
757. - 30
758. - 3200
759. - 350
760. - 75
761. - 650 if perfect
762. - 175
763. - 50
764. - 75
765. - 65
766. - 85
767. - 325
768. - 150
769. - 300
770. - 75
771. - 650
772. - 75
773. - 125
774. - 175
775. - 175
776. - 175
777. - 175

778. - 85
779. - 85
780. - 85
781. - 650
782. - 200
783. - 225
784. - 50
785. - 50
786. - 50
787. - 50
788. - 45 ea.
789. - 150
790. - 200
791. - 350
792. - 450
793. - 325
794. - 350
795. - 950 set
796. - w/#795
797. - w/#795
798. - 125
799. - 2000
800. - 2000
801. - 600 set
802. - w/#801
803. - 1500
804. - 450
805. - 550
806. - 175
807. - 175
808. - 750
809. - 800
810. - 2000
811. - 250
812. - 450
813. - 1200
814. - 1600
815. - 1500
816. - 550
817. - 1600
818. - 150
819. - 350
820. - 100
821. - 550
822. - 300
823. - 275
824. - 300
825. - 350
826. - 150
827. - 100
828. - 150
829. - 150

830. - 2200 w/correct stopper
831. - 2000
832. - 1000
833. - no photo
834. - 1200
835. - 3200
836. - 750
837. - 1200
838. - 200
839. a. - 225
     b. - 150
840. - 1250
841. - 150
842. a. - 150
     b. - 75
     c. - 100
843. a. - 1850
     b. - 2850
     c. - 2250
844. a. - 850
     b. - 1750
     c. - 950
     d. - 875
845. a. - 1500
     b. - 1850
     c. - 1800
846. - 1250
847. - 950
848. - 1850
849. - 1250
850. - 1650
851. - 1850
852. a. - 1450
     b. - 1250
     c. - 3200
     tray - 950
853. - N/A
854. front row
     a. - 1450
     b. - 1550
     c. - 1650
     d. - 1550
     back row
     a. - 825
     b. - 1850
     c. - 950
855. a. - 1850
     b. - 1650
856. a. - 2250
     b. - 1650
857. a. - 2250

     b. - 1650
     c. - 1250
858. a. - 1250
     b. - 1500
     c. - 1800
859. - N/A
860. - N/A
861 - 870. 34 - 225 depending on color and style.
871. - N/A
872. - 1800
873. - 1900
874. - 1200
875. - 1500
876. - 900
877. - 1100
878. - 1100
879. - 1200
880. - 1200
881. - 1800
882. - 1400
883. - 2600
884. - 3000
885. - 1800
886. - 1100
887. - 1200
888. - 1200
889. - 2500
890. - N/A
891. - 3800
892. - 1900
893. - 2500
894. - 1500
895. - 1800
896. a. - 950
     b. - 3000
897. - 2500
898. - 1900
899. - N/A
900. - N/A
901. - N/A
902. - 2800
903. - N/A
904. - N/A
905. - N/A

NOTES

NOTES

NOTES

NOTES